LOCAL CHURCH

LOCAL CHURCH

LOVE IT; LEAVE IT; CHANGE IT.

RICK THOMAS

LOCAL CHURCH:
Love It; Leave It; Change It.

ISBN 978-1-7323854-8-1

Rick Thomas

© 2025 Life Over Coffee

Unless otherwise noted, all Scripture references herein are from the English Standard Version, copyright © 2001 by Crossway, Inc. Used by permission. All rights reserved.

No part of this publication may be reproduced, stored in a retrieval system, or transmitted in any form or by any means without the express written permission of Life Over Coffee.

Edited by Sarah Hayhurst

Life Over Coffee
8595 Pelham Rd Ste 400 #406,
Greenville, SC 29615
LifeOverCoffee.com

Dedication

To the church and their pastors who shepherd them.

Obey your leaders and submit to them, for they are keeping watch over your souls, as those who will have to give an account. Let them do this with joy and not with groaning, for that would be of no advantage to you.

(Hebrews 13:17)

For additional resources, visit lifeovercoffee.com

Table of Contents

Introduction 8
1 Why Do You Attend? 10
2 What Kind of Church? 18
3 The Main Thing 26
4 Second Most Important Thing 34
5 Three Fantastic Characteristics 42
6 Qualities of a Pastor 50
7 Signs of Spiritual Abuse 60
8 Preaching or Discipleship 70
9 Need More Than Preaching 78
10 A Perfect Dysfunctional Place 86
11 A Crazy Idea 94
12 Do You Fight Fires? 104
13 Are You Committed? 114
14 The Church Won't Help 124
15 How Do You Leave? 132
16 Does He Groan? 140
About the Author 144

Introduction

What do you think about your local church? Do you love it? Great! Maybe you want to leave it? That is an option. Have you thought about changing it? Perhaps you have thought about that but are not sure how.

Let me suggest that before you do anything else, read this book. I cover a lot of bases and answer a ton of questions. I will challenge you about why you attend your church. I also spend some time assessing the leadership of your church. And some chapters will press you to engage more effectively. The goals of this book are straightforward. Here are my top three:

1. I hope to spread the fame of God through this work.
2. I hope to encourage and guide church leadership.
3. I hope to envision and equip the body of Christ.

As far as a community is concerned, the local church is the dearest place on earth. It's our preaching center and sanctification hospital. It's the place where the followers of Christ gather to worship our Leader and build up each other. There is nothing like it in our fallen world. May the Lord use this book to help you make your local church a better community for His glory and your benefit.

—Rick

1

Why Do You Attend?

One of the most important questions you'll ever ask yourself is why you attend your church. Outside the family unit, the local church is the primary context where sanctification happens among Christians, making how we think about and participate in our local churches crucial. Assuming you're part of a local church, why do you attend? Perhaps you're part of the de-church movement; if so, why have you stopped attending a local church?

Break a Leg

In 1988, my then-wife committed adultery and left our nine-year marriage. She subsequently divorced me in 1991. During the first year of the separation, no one from my church contacted me or came alongside me to assist in any way. In one day, I lost my wife and two children, an irreparable breach in a family. After the first year of solitude, I went to my assistant pastor of this 1,200-member church and asked him why no one in any leadership capacity had come alongside me, inquired about me, or tried to help me through the most challenging time of my life. My separation and subsequent divorce were well-known in our church because I was well-known.

The assistant pastor responded by saying, "You did not break your leg." Though it was awkward, I appreciated his words—in a sense. They were honest, and he was transparent. He explained that if I had broken my leg, the church would have known what to do because they knew how to send flowers, prepare meals, give money, and visit hospitals. They did not know what to do with someone like me. After a moment of reflection, I impulsively responded, "Please let me know if you encounter someone in a similar situation because I know what to do." My response to him was more arrogant than honest. The truth was that I did not have a clue what to do. I could not help myself, let alone help anyone else. I was no different from the church I was hoping would help me.

I have not shared this story with you because I am angry. I am not mad. I have not shared this story with you because I am bitter or have an axe to grind. I have not shared this story to mentally manipulate you to anger. I share this story with you because you need to know my worldview regarding the local church. You need to understand my soul care presuppositions. I cannot detach myself from my worldview or presuppositions any more than I can stop being a Christian. I spent the next twelve years learning how to do soul care, mainly on me because I did not know how to disciple myself. What I did not know was that God was writing a grander script to create a long-form narrative for how I would spend the rest of my life.

My passion for sharing the life-changing message of the gospel was born out of a broken heart restored by God and redeemed for His fame.

—Rick Thomas

Preaching Centers

My pastor and the other leaders of our large church did not know how to do soul care. They could not take a broken-down Christian and walk him through the transformational steps to be whole again. They could not provide the transformational contexts for the congregation to receive and provide soul care. It is a miracle that God restored me despite my ignorance and the inability of our local church. My experience is the point of the question I asked at the beginning: why do you attend your church? My concern is that most believers have insufficient or even selfish reasons for their church attendance, which is part of why church attendance is declining.

In 2001, a well-known Christian leader asked me why I was a member of the church I attended at that time. I said, "Because of the preaching." He did not respond to my answer, but I have never forgotten his question, which has been rolling around in my brain ever since. If you asked anyone in the large church I attended in 1988 why they participated in that church, nearly everyone would have said because of the preaching. That church was a preaching center; it was not a discipleship community. It was a famous church—within their circle of churches—for preaching. At one point, it was the king of the hill when it came to popularity, a popularity built upon the personality and preaching style of the preacher.

Today, it is a congregational shell, held together by a handful of gray-haired loyalists and a few zealots. Back then, my church was vibrant. We were doing ministry worldwide, but when it came to soul problems and soul care, we could not help each other because we did not know how. The truth is that the pastor was a spiritual abuser with a gift for preaching. That church and that pastor are not abnormal. I have seen this scenario play out hundreds of times with individuals, couples, and families. I'm not speaking of abuse per se, but insufficient soul care practices. Nearly all of these hurting souls were part of conservative, evangelical, Bible-believing, and doctrinally sound churches. It is similar to a hospital with the best equipment, but the doctors and staff lack the training to help the hurting.

Gospel Transformation

If your first response to why you attend your church is the preaching, I appeal to you to rethink why you attend. Your first reason must be better than that. Preaching is vital, but we can go beyond being the best preaching center in town. Where would folks place the accent mark in your church? Is it more of a preaching center, a discipleship community, or something else? Each church has an emphasis which creates the appeal.

The best spot on the ecclesiastical spectrum to place the accent mark is on the gospel. The purpose of Christ's—the gospel—coming was to transform people, which begins at salvation and continues through progressive sanctification until every believer experiences glorification in heaven. Being born again does not bring complete sanctification. Our salvation is a point-in-time, nonrepeatable event. Like walking into a fitness center for the first time, it gets you in the door, but it does not transform you. Progressive sanctification is our daily working out of salvation (Philippians 2:12–13). The primary contexts are our homes and our local churches.

> *Progressive transformation is weak in many churches, and because some churches don't sufficiently address this problem, some of God's children are unnecessarily struggling.*
> —Rick Thomas

I praise God for fantastic preaching, but you do not have

enough if that is all you have. The last few years have seen good preaching and good preachers rise and fall. They built their local congregations on one person's personality, and the church fell proportionally when he fell. There has been a lot of cyber talk about why these ministries and preachers crumbled. The reason is simple: they did not do sanctification well, starting with themselves. Poor sanctification practices will eventually manifest in a person, marriage, family, and organization. It almost always goes that way, which makes assessing the problem somewhat straightforward.

Sheep Analysis

One of the ways you can discern how well your leadership understands and practices sanctification is by evaluating the condition of the sheep. If the church people are not well cared for in their sanctification, it points to deficiencies within the leadership to provide that care. (I am not speaking of regular attendees, visitors, on any other person or family that has yet committed to the church or does actively engage it.) This problem may be more serious than you imagine. Each local church is a reflection of the leadership, good or bad. You cannot provide for others what you do not possess yourself. You may be able to impress the masses for a while, but ultimately, there is no discontinuity between what you are and what you do (Luke 6:45); thus, what you are will affect those around you.

Suppose a large sample size of the church is not appropriately cared for. It could be that the growth happened because of the preaching. Great! Now, what's the plan to care for those you have drawn in through fantastic preaching? Is there a plan to care for these sheep? Perhaps there needs to be a deeper conversation within the leadership about their personal, marital, and familial practices of sanctification as well as how they are exporting those practices to the sheep God has called them to shepherd. This perspective is a similar conversation with parents who bring rebellious children to me for counseling. It is rare for a teen to be so messed up and confused without negative shaping influences from the parents. There can be exceptions to this, but they are exceptions only, not the norm.

Who we are directly impacts our spheres of influence, and if our churches are not doing well in sanctification, the first thing to address is not more programs or small group initiatives. The wiser move would be to look at the leadership to assess their personal lives, marriages, and families. I'm not suggesting their families are walking with God because God grants repentance, not the leader. However, you want to discern a leader's sanctification competence. Are the pastors vulnerable, transparent, honest, and accountable with their lives and marriages? Are the pastors and wives mutually and reciprocally discipling each other? Are they able to walk each other through their relational problems? There are other reasons a church does not do soul care well, but you must not avoid the leadership's sanctification responsibilities and practices.

Call to Action

You go to your doctor because you believe that they can help you. You go to your mechanic because you trust that he can diagnose and repair your vehicle. You go to your dentist because you have faith that he will be able to preserve your teeth. Are your pastors and their wives authentically pursuing a sanctified life together? How do you know? Can your pastors walk you through your relational and situational challenges? Who do you call when things go wrong in your life or relationships? Are you confident your church can provide what you need to mature in your sanctification?

When your life takes a turn you did not anticipate and your heart breaks, is your church your sanctification center

LOCAL CHURCH

of choice? If you are not calling on your pastors (or the contexts and the means they provide) to walk you through your problems, you must reconsider why you attend that church. I have spoken to many Christians about these matters. One of the most common responses they share is their church's weakness in doing soul care. I understand their dilemma, and if it is true for you, here are some suggestions for your consideration.

1. **MAKE A DIFFERENCE:** Do not choose anger or other divisive responses to this problem. Do not complain about what your church is not. Begin praying about how you can be part of the solution.
2. **HAVE A CONVERSATION:** Talk to a leader in your church. Start humbly and compassionately stirring the pot (Hebrews 10:25). Do not let the conversation die. Draw attention to the problems you perceive. You can do this in non-divisive ways (Ephesians 4:29).
3. **TRAIN YOURSELF:** If you do not know how to walk an adult through an addiction, a wife through the adultery of her husband, or a teen through the hurt of an angry dad, learn how to disciple. You are welcome to explore our Mastermind Program, which you can complete online.
4. **IMMEDIATELY IMPLEMENT:** Do not wait until you think you can bring care to another person. Your skill will come with your practice. The woman at the well told all she knew at that time. She did not wait until she became a Greek scholar to care for others.

I ignorantly told my pastor that if anyone came to him with a problem and he did not know how to help, let me know. I suppose it was a good thought, but I had no clue how to help anyone, especially myself. My response to him set me on a course to learn how to do more than lead someone to Christ.

You can do it too. You do not have to be church-dependent. If your church is not going to change or does not know how to change, you change yourself and then become a means of grace to assist your church.

2

What Kind of Church?

Each local church has a unique personality that reflects its leadership. In context, the word church refers to those who have been attending for a while and are actively participating in the environments and equipping ministries that the leadership provides. Nominal Christians or inconsistent attendees are not part of the demographic in view here. Because of the leaders' influence, assessing the church's model for ministry is vital because no two leaders are the same, making no two churches the same. Let's examine six standard church models by looking at their upsides and downsides.

Needs and Preferences

Perhaps recognizing that every church should not be the same is the best way to begin this discussion. It would be sad if all churches were identical because people, cultures, regions, trends, and eras differ. The devastating effect of multiculturalism is the belief that you can bring the world together as one collective, and we will get along. This worldview defies the purpose of God for confounding the languages in Genesis 11 as well as the total depravity of humanity, kicking off in Genesis 3:6. God does not want us to think and act as one because we cannot be trusted to play well with each other. Trying to create heaven on earth is the errand of fools. The wise person recognizes the upside of diversity, that we are different, and segmenting ourselves off from—certain—others is wise. Even our dating apps have compatibility assessments because they know people polarize.

However, finding a good local church that meets a Christian's season of life, family dynamics, and preferences can be challenging. Because our preferences are so broad, it would be impossible for one church to accommodate all the flavors the core membership desires, though there are non-negotiables: the gospel is front and center (Philippians 1:15–18; Galatians 1:8–9). Sound theology is another vital need that no biblical church can survive without. A church should continually grow in their theological precision. Perhaps you would add humble, Christ-emulating, non-lording shepherds to your list of non-negotiables. Most everything else is a preference.

> Shepherd the flock of God that is among you, exercising oversight, not under compulsion, but willingly, as God would have you; not for shameful gain, but eagerly; not domineering over those in your charge, but being examples to the flock.
> (1 Peter 5:2–3)

I have listed six of the more typical church styles. I will assume all of them preach the gospel, lean toward theological precision, and are led by humble shepherds. They all have their place in the Christian landscape, though you will probably prefer one over the other, depending on your walk with God, your season of life, and what you consider more preferential in a local church.

1: Seeker

The seeker church is a group that desires a relevant connection to its culture and proximate communities. To do this, it learns how to cater to the culture's palate. Some have even surveyed the culture to create what they like within the church environment. These churches have drawing power if they do their homework. Many people enjoy this kind of church life. The upside is they are excellent on the front end, drawing people to the church to give them the gospel. The downside is that they overemphasize relating to their culture, which weakens their theological education and practical equipping of its members. The people can be deficient in living out progressive sanctification to a great extent. If the seeker church endures, it will plateau quickly because the learning environments and expectations for holiness have a low ceiling. Because spiritual stagnation is common, the back door will become as busy as the front door as folks who want to mature will leave, creating a transient environment of unregenerate, nominal, novice, and growing believers left behind.

2: Do-over

One of the most popular kinds of church is comprised of people burned out by a former less desirable church experience. This demographic seeks something different from their pasts and gravitates toward a refreshing, vibrant church culture. People from heretical church environments or legalistic cultures are perfect for this kind of church. They recognized the heresy or grew weary of the restrictive legalism. A church like this will make much of grace, even to their detriment. If you ask them why they attend their church, you will hear repeated themes:

- "I have never heard the Bible preached like this before."
- "I do not feel judged when I walk through the doors of this church."
- "This church is not about rule-keeping."
- "I never understood grace until I came here."
- "The worship experience is alive and authentic."

Nearly all of the good things they say are framed in comparative language—aligning their current church experience with their past experience. They love the do-over opportunity because their former church experience became a heavy yoke that accelerated joylessness, even tempting them to sin by grumbling, judging, cynicism, and despair. Their new church moves the theological needle more toward soundness than cultural relevance or legalistic smothering. The people typically have more Bible knowledge but have difficulty letting go of the past. You can take the fundamentalist out of fundamentalism, but it's hard to remove the characteristics of fundamentalism from the expat.

3: Evangelistic

Some churches do a fantastic job reaching the lost locally and globally. They want to go into the world with the gospel and do it exemplarily. As you leave their auditoriums, you may read a sign that says, «You are now entering the mission field.» Like seeker and do-over churches, they focus more on the outward mission field than the inward mission field of each member's heart. The seeker relates to their pagan culture but is weak in maturing within the church. The do-over group relates well to the burned-out religious people but is also weak in discipleship. The evangelistic folks know how to win people to Christ but are not so good with sanctification issues. In each of these demographics, you'll notice a reactionary attitude among them. The backward look to where they came from continues to manage them as they move on with their lives.

4: Ministry

These ministry-minded people are busy doing everything for their community and the world. Like ants scurrying around an ant hill, these Christians know how to get things done for Jesus. I am not talking about a social gospel. These are missional Christians who are on a genuine quest for Jesus. The leadership is adept at providing ministry opportunities for their people. All you need is a burden to start your unique ministry. If the church does not have a ministry that matches your burden, they will figure out how to spin you up because they want the world to know about Jesus. Ministries are portals to reach the world. The downside is similar to the previously mentioned sanctification problems with the other models. This group is too busy to slow down to do expert soul care. They are ministry-minded, even to the detriment of their marriages and families. Character does not rank high when they assess a person for ministry duties. You can be an unkind spouse or ill-equipped parent and still lead a ministry. A person's passion for ministry carries more weight than Christlike character qualifications.

5: Educated

This people group loves to study their Bibles. They have an endless supply of Bible studies for every demographic within the church. Knowledge is king. They are correct that being theologically sound is the essential prerequisite to growing in sanctification. The downside is that growing in sanctification requires more than Bible knowledge. They do not match their penchant for the Bible with an equal, appropriate, and practical application of the Bible. One of the more incongruent things with many Christians, who know a lot about the Bible, is they do not know how to walk a person, or even themselves, through critical sanctification issues. The gulf between what they know and how to practically apply it to a struggling person's life can be broad. Like the previous models, eventually, you are tempted to leave this kind of environment because you want practical help that transforms lives. Building taller silos to store more Bible knowledge is not the answer when your life, marriage, family, or community is spiraling into ever-increasing dysfunction.

6: Disciplers

Disciplemakers are probably the rarest group because it is the most challenging aspect of our religion to accomplish. Creating contexts where people are honest, transparent, intrusive, humble, compassionate, courageous, and able to practicalize the gospel into personal problems and situational challenges is a bridge too far for many churches. To take a couple, a single, or a teen through relational difficulty in the context of a local church is the exception rather than the rule. Our inability to replicate Christ in people's lives is perplexing in light of Peter and Paul's expectations for God's Word. (See 2 Peter 1:3-4; 2 Timothy 2:2, 3:16-17.) The Lord's intent for sanctification is to happen in a community of competent and compassionate Christlike disciple-makers. The downside of this group is that it may lead to ingrown stagnation if it does not do some of the things the other groups are doing. However, this model best represents a New Testament church because it preaches sound theology and creates equipping contexts to apply it within the milieus of the local church. If it also reaches its community and the world, it's as good as a church can be.

Sheep and Shepherds

Which one do you like? If you are like me, I suspect you enjoy a combination of all the models. You want to be biblically relevant. Jesus was. You want to be evangelistic, missional, and ministry-minded, for sure. You also want to grow in your faith. These are all good things for a local body, so how do you decide? If the gospel is correct and the theology is precise, what kind of imperfect church will you call home? Factoring imperfection into your church experience is essential. If you do not, you will be disappointed. All local churches are full of imperfect people. The whole is a collection of its parts. If the parts are unclean, which they are, the whole will experience traces of uncleanness. To expect otherwise will tempt the Christian to leave their church for the wrong reasons. Say this aloud: there is no perfect church. If the gospel is sound, if the theological depth is deepening, if the imperfections are not too glaring, if transformation is happening, one of the most important questions you can ask regarding the church you want to attend is, "Who do I want to shepherd me?"

> Obey your leaders and submit to them, for they are keeping watch over your souls, as those who will have to give an account. Let them do this with joy and not with groaning, for that would be of no advantage to you.
>
> (Hebrews 13:17)

The church you attend will reflect its lead pastor in many ways. His life and vision will be the primary imprint, unfolding into a combination of the models presented. The question for you is whether or not you can follow him as he follows Christ while accepting the vision he believes is suitable for this local assembly. His vision will directly and practically impact your life and those under your responsibility. Perhaps thinking through the shepherding question with these questions will assist. Who do you want to follow? Who do you want to affect you? Who do you want to influence your spouse, children, and friends? Let's say you are married, and your spouse has a relational or situational difficulty. Can your shepherd shepherd you? Does your shepherd know how to provide care for you and your spouse?

Suppose you have a teenager who is struggling with sin. Can your youth leader/pastor walk you and your child through this challenging season? Who do you call when you need a practical shepherd's care? The church should reach the lost and create ministry portals so more people can hear the good news about Jesus. The church must be a sanctification hospital for its members. If the church cannot care for its wounded, those who march under that church's banner are in the wrong place. It would be like a company saying, "We can do [such and such] for you." After you buy their product, you realize they cannot fulfill their promises. Your salvation is much more than being born again. Regeneration is the beginning of your journey with God and others. If your best efforts get people in the door but cannot provide practical sanctification care, you must re-evaluate your priorities and your local church.

Call to Action

1. What kind of church do you attend? Perhaps it's a blend of the models above. How would you describe it?
2. Why do you attend your church? What compels you to be part of this local body of believers?
3. How does your church need to change—as you think charitably about your church?
4. What unique gifts do you have that make your church more effective, and how are you employing them? Are you part of the solution that your church needs?

3

The Main Thing

The local church is our most crucial sanctification context outside our homes, making finding the right kind of church a critical matter for all serious-minded Christians. The church search can be daunting because there are so many varieties, and we have a plethora of preferences. If you were to highlight a few essentials of things you'd like for your church to be, what would be on your list? More specifically, what is the main thing you want when looking for a place to mature in Christ, care for others, spread the fame of God throughout your community, and glorify our heavenly Father?

The Main Thing

It happens. Whether you want it to happen or not, it will probably happen to you. It seems to be more the rule than the exception. There was a time when hardly anyone left their churches. But in our transient culture, our spoiled natures, and pastoral mishandling of the Word of God, it is the rule. People and churches don't stay together like when the world was smaller and the options were limited. I certainly fall into this category. A few years ago, we looked for another church to attend. Looking for a local church is on my top ten list of things I don't want to do. Leaving friends, making new friends, and finding our place in a new environment was daunting. But we went through it. That season challenged us to think through how we valued the local church—mainly, what we believed was essential for our family.

If you were looking for a local church to join, what are the main things on your list? What is important to you? What are your non-negotiables? These are huge questions, and how you answer them will affect you and your family for years and generations. Our criteria for settling in a mature and sound local church boiled down to five things. I did not want to make a list so long that no church would qualify. There are no perfect churches. Therefore, we developed a list that covered five main areas of the Christian life. In this chapter, I will speak to the first one, the gospel—the main thing, and develop the others in the succeeding chapters.

1. **Gospel:** the main thing
2. **Theology:** the foundation of our lives
3. **Worship:** expressing gratitude to God privately and corporately
4. **Fellowship:** various contexts to mature into Christlikeness
5. **Ministries:** contexts to serve others, using our unique gifts

Gospel Transcendence

I trust the easy part regarding the main thing when selecting a church is the gospel. Though there are many preferences that we want to elevate, nothing transcends the vitalness and value of the gospel. Paul said if anyone preached another gospel other than the gospel he preached, that person should be accursed (Galatians 1:6-9). We cannot say that about music, children's ministry, or other essential preferences. Paul's elevation of the gospel settled the "what's the number one thing you look for in a church" question. For example, Paul flexed on whether we should eat meat but did not bend on the gospel (1 Corinthians 8:1-13). And we know why because in Romans 1:16, he said, "For I am not ashamed of the gospel, for it is the power of God for salvation to everyone who believes."

Paul saw the gospel as the power of salvation and the power for sanctification (Ephesians 4-6). According to his theology, the authority appropriated through the gospel affects every area of our lives. Peter agreed. Will you appreciate these inspiring words about the gospel? "His divine power has granted to us all things that pertain to life and godliness, through the knowledge of him who called us to his glory and excellence" (2 Peter 1:3). As convincing as Paul and Peter were about the preeminence of the gospel, it was not their perspectives that put it at the top of my list. The gospel—Christ—is the Bible's most significant message to humanity.

The Old Testament writers pointed to the person and work of Christ. The New Testament writers explained the person and work of Christ. Eternity is the unending place where we will worship the person and work of Christ. Believers in the best local churches purposely center themselves on the gospel—the person and work of Christ. He is the One who matters the most. John the Baptist was necessary for a while. Then he went away. The apostles stepped in for a season. They left too. The gospel is the only transcending, unmovable fixture in our lives (other than the Word of God). Christ is the beginning and end of all we do.

Gospel Centerpiece

Draw a circle in the middle of a piece of paper. Inside that circle, you write the word gospel—or Christ. Now, draw lines from Christ to any spot on the paper and write a word at the end of the line, e.g., family, finances, vocation, health, hobbies, friends, sanctification, repentance, forgiveness, joy, etc. That's the idea. Christ is the centerpiece who connects to every aspect of our lives. Everything in life flows from this gospel-centered worldview. Unfortunately, some churches place other things in the center of the circle, which is how they are known, e.g., The Second-Chance Church. Whatever becomes your primary focus will become your identity. Every church has a central theme.

- Some churches are ministry-centered.
- Some churches are theology-centered.
- Some churches are casualness-centered.
- Some churches focus on the down and out.
- Some churches are charismatic-centered.
- Some churches make grace the main thing.
- Some churches react to what they are not any longer.

A church is similar to a Christian in that we all have an identity. The Christian's identity should be Jesus Christ—the gospel. We take on His alien righteousness, His characteristics. We become Christlike. The local church is full of Christlike followers, which is why a local church's identity is Christ (or it should be). A church without Christ as its identity will teach their people to make something else the center of their lives. Perhaps the best way to discern the heart of a church is to discover what they emphasize the most. Is it great preaching? Is it the preacher? What is the main thing? That thing pushes all other things—including Christ—to the periphery. My appeal to anyone looking for a local church is to determine if Christ is the centerpiece of all they do. Heaven is a place with Christ in the center, and wisdom implies Christians should prep for heaven today by making Him the centerpiece of our lives.

> Then I looked, and I heard around the throne and the living creatures and the elders the voice of many angels, numbering myriads of myriads and thousands of thousands, saying with a loud voice,

> "Worthy is the Lamb who was slain, to receive power and wealth and wisdom and might and honor and glory and blessing!" And I heard every creature in heaven and on earth and under the earth and in the sea, and all that is in them, saying, "To him who sits on the throne and to the Lamb be blessing and honor and glory and might forever and ever!" And the four living creatures said, "Amen!" and the elders fell and worshiped.
> (Revelation 5:11–14)

Gospel Transformation

The gospel brings you into a transformative experience with Christ. The only way to change is by having a dynamic relationship with Jesus. It's this necessity that makes gospel-centered teaching more important than things like a principle-driven life. Principles teach you how to relate to Christ, but principles without Christ will not transform you. They are bumper stickers or social media quotes that drip dopamine. Best practices are similar as they temporarily shape your life according to the proportion and degree you use them. Tips provide light. They may inspire. But principles and practices were never meant to bring sustainable, inside to outside, transformation. Bible seminars and weekend retreats are inspiring; men's meetings are terrific. Programs, initiatives, Bible nuggets, and your latest favorite book can lift you over a hurdle.

There is a place for all these things in Christendom, but if the gospel is not the centerpiece of our lives, we will always need these religious puffs like a chain smoker needs another cigarette. Without a dynamic, interactive relationship with Jesus, we're only as strong as our latest principle, book, or conference. The secular world provides principles, books, and conferences. We have Jesus. Principles and programs, as effective as they may be, are analogous to the parts of a car. The gospel, on the other hand, is the engine that makes everything go. The issue here is not this or that but about priority and preeminence. The gospel is at the heart of the Christian life.

Go back to the circle in the middle of the paper. What is at the epicenter of your life? If it's Christ, you're in a great place, and you'll long for a church that makes much of Christ. I'm not suggesting that every sermon makes a beeline to Christ and stays there, but He must always be the flavor of the day, even as we exegete and teach other passages that do not speak to the centrality of Christ. The goal is for every Christian to fall in love with Jesus, and out of that great affection for what He has done and is doing, we find the motivation to obey Him in all things, perseverance during our harshest trials, and an unencumbered desire to tell others they can refresh their souls with the water He gives (John 4:14).

Gospel Applied

Our search for a new church started with understanding the church's view and practice of the gospel. The two most important questions were: "Does the church have a sound view of the gospel?" We answered that question by asking this one: "How is the gospel actively presented to and practically changing the church?" We were not looking for a church that had perfected its understanding of the gospel. Gospel transformation is always a work in progress. We were looking for evidence that the church understands how to practically implement the gospel into their lives, which is why these follow-up questions were essential.

- Is the gospel transforming the leadership?
- Are they transparent and open about their struggles?
- Are they establishing the baseline for confession?
- How does the gospel motivate them to live so that

the congregation can learn from their successes and failures?
- Are their spouses being transformed similarly?
- Are the marriages of the leadership something you want to export to the congregation?
- Would it be in the congregation's best interest to follow the leadership because of how they follow the gospel?
- How has the exported gospel impacted the people in the church?
- How has the heart of the leadership become the heart of the people?
- How is the gospel influencing and directing the programs and ministries of the church?

If we are rightly affected by the gospel, then we have nothing to fear, nothing to protect, and nothing to hide. The gospel sets the captive free, releasing him to become everything God intends for him to become. The gospel becomes the centerpiece, attaching and affecting every area of our lives. It becomes evident to others that the animating center is Christ, and the gospel contagion grows. The disciples of Christ were affected by Christ, and they turned the world on its head. That's how it works. Disciples follow Christ, creating a gravitational pull that compels others to follow them as they follow Christ (1 Corinthians 11:1), making the church's leadership assessment question valid and valuable when seeing if a church has the gospel as its theme. The gospel is not an ethereal, vague idea but rather a practical life you want to emulate.

Call to Action

1. Why is the gospel the main thing you want to see in your church?
2. If you believe something else is more important, what is it, and will you make a case for it?
3. How have you centered your life on the gospel, and what practical evidence would support your gospel-centered life?
4. Will you work through the ten questions I asked about the church and its leadership to adapt and apply them to yourself? I would not want to assess my leaders without considering myself first. It would be disingenuous to expect them to be something I'm not striving to become. Perhaps speaking with a close friend about those ten questions would help clarify your strengths and weaknesses in applying the gospel to your life.

4

Second Most Important Thing

The most important question when looking for a local church concerns the gospel—the main thing forever and ever. Amen. Nothing is more essential in any local church than the good news of the gospel, who is Christ. So, let's suppose we exalt Christ in our minds and seek to imitate Him in all we do. If so, it will create a presuppositional window to interpret our theology, worship, ministries, and everything else in church life is congruent with the gospel we exalt. To follow Christ well implies that we will disregard anything that will impede or hinder our walk with Him. Thus, with Christ established as the preeminent one, we have the proper filter to discern the other vital matters of the church.

Gospel Established

> But even if we or an angel from heaven should preach to you a gospel contrary to the one we preached to you, let him be accursed. As we have said before, so now I say again: If anyone is preaching to you a gospel contrary to the one you received, let him be accursed.
>
> (Galatians 1:8–9)

The gospel is the person and work of Jesus Christ—His person (ontology) and His activity (function), the most vital aspects in our lives, too. Who we are and what we do are connected (Luke 6:45). Thus, our state of being (ontology) must be like Jesus so that our works can be like Jesus. If the church properly understands and practices the gospel— Christ, it positions itself to equip each other in our ongoing transformation into the Christ, which is what I mean by a presupposition to interpret all of life; we have gospelized glasses that provide discernment to pick and choose the most biblically precise way to live.

> Some indeed preach Christ from envy and rivalry, but others from good will. The latter do it out of love, knowing that I am put here for the defense of the gospel. The former proclaim Christ out of selfish ambition, not sincerely but thinking to afflict me in my imprisonment. What then? Only that in every way, whether in pretense or in truth, Christ is proclaimed, and in that I rejoice.
> (Philippians 1:15-18)

For several years, I had the opportunity of being part of a local church's pastoral team. One of my responsibilities was to follow up with our guests. In many cases, I was the first contact our guests heard from after their initial visit. Our local church had over 3,000 first-time guests during the five years that I kept track. I fielded thousands of questions about our church. The one question never asked was our church's view of the gospel. Never. Literally. No one was interested in how we thought about the gospel or how we sought to practicalize Him in the lives of our local body. Perhaps they assumed we were right on the gospel. Maybe they were unaware that we could not imitate Him properly without a clear understanding of Christ (Ephesians 5:1; 1 Corinthians 11:1; Philippians 4:9). I don't know, but what

I do know is the things that were most important to them were almost always tertiary matters.

The Second Question

Questions like, "Tell me about children's ministry," "What kind of music do you all have," and "What other ministries do you offer?" All of these queries are important, but they don't rank that high on the list and most certainly do not come close to the importance of the gospel. Sometimes, our newcomers would inquire about the second most crucial question when looking for the church: its theology. The gospel and theology are like 1a and 1b. They are two inseparable parts of a whole that determine the kind of church you belong to. Christ is the elevated example you worship, the pattern your life imitates, and your theology brings Him into perfect view. With Christ lifted and our theology informing how we think about Him, we're in the best place to practically live Him out in our communities.

To those who spend their lives helping Christians through personal, relational, and situational problems, it's unsurprising to them that the view of the gospel and theological positions of the fellow strugglers they help are secondary matters at best. These folks tend toward pragmatism: What's in it for me? How can you help me? There is a clear correlation between a person's views about the gospel and theology and how they practically live their Christian lives. Without clarity about the person and work of Jesus Christ and sound theology, you cannot live a sound, practical Christian life. Theology implies the primary doctrines of the faith: Bibliology, Theology Proper, Christology, Pneumatology, Anthropology, Hamartiology, Soteriology, Ecclesiology, etc. Perhaps a few questions will help you evaluate where you stand regarding your theology. Please use the Theological Pyramid to create those questions to examine your view and practice of theology.

Second Most Important Thing

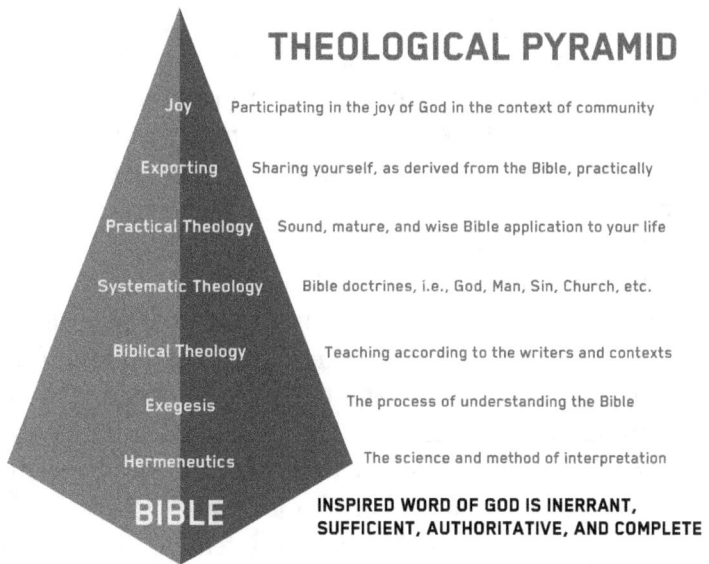

Everyone is theological. Everyone has a view and practice of God in their lives. Satan has a theology: he adamantly rejects God. Your church reveals its theology about their mastery of God's Word, the primary source material to build a theological framework. They shape your thoughts about theology and influence how you apply theology to your life and world. Outside your family, the local church is the most essential theological shaping influence in any Christian's life. Perhaps this visual of our Theological Pyramid will assist in understanding the structure and process for living a gospel-centered life.

Preferences Matter

The questions about preferences that I asked earlier do matter. I have preferences about my local church's music, children's ministry, and other ministries because I care about our church's values, practices, and how they will care for my family. You care too. But in another sense, it does not amount to a hill of beans what kind of music a church plays or the comprehensiveness of its ministries if they have skewed views of the gospel and theology. There is a prioritization sequence that is vital: the gospel and theology come before and set the stage for everything that follows. If the church is not right on the gospel, it won't be right in its theology or whatever else it may provide, and it will fall woefully short of God's Word.

I have listened to Roman Catholic music that is hands down better than some of the music in Baptist churches I have attended. I'm not going to join a Roman Catholic church because I disagree with their theology. The Mormon church has some fabulous music too. They also have a high view of the family as their video resources impressively present. But their theology is abysmal. The Jehovah Witnesses can shame most Christians in their ministry zeal, particularly in the area of community outreach. But we know better. There is no sound theological argument for becoming a Jehovah Witness. A local church can provide the most amazing accoutrements of religion but not give you a theologically sound and practically replicable Jesus.

Preferences are essential, but our preferences may be detrimental to our souls without a clear understanding of the gospel or sound theology. One of the most effective ways to determine your motive for being part of your church is by answering why you attend your church. If your primary motive concerns a preference rather than (1a) the gospel and (1b) sound theology, I appeal to you to reconsider why you belong to your church. Let me provide you with a list of secondary preferences that should never come before 1a and 1b: music genre, Bible versions, children's ministries, a place to fulfill your burden, preaching style, programs, and outreach. You can do nearly all of those things in a secular organization or in a church with awful theology and a zero understanding of the gospel. But what do you have? Without a high and lifted-up gospel, informed by sound theology, you're in a local church that will not give you what you need.

Can't Find One

The assumption is that gospel-sound and theologically precise churches are everywhere, especially in America. It's not true, and it's worse in other countries where the gospel has never been or left centuries ago. In areas where there is a shortage of gospel exaltation and sound theology, the good news is that there are more options today than in the past. They are not as preferable, but God will not forsake you even if you cannot gather as a local church. In most places worldwide, internet access puts you seconds away from pastors and churches doing it the right way. Of course, the internet creates an ease-of-access temptation for those with disappointing church experiences. I understand this temptation in the most painful of ways as I was part of Sovereign Grace Ministries, an authoritarian, abusive, and corrupt organization that could have been the impetus for me to never set foot in a local church again.

It took me two years to recover from what happened during my tenure with Sovereign Grace. However, we had a church option in our community during that time, and we took it. I would appeal to anyone who has had a horrible church experience not to let what happened to you sour your view of God's church. Be honest with yourself, and though the choice in your area might not be the most favorable, if they are right on the gospel and practice sound theology, become part of that gathering and make a difference. The response to bad experiences is not retreating, isolating, and walling yourself off from a primary means of grace that God's Word puts forth to help us mature through the fallenness of our world, especially if the disappointment comes from the church.

Other folks have chosen house churches and smaller gatherings of like-minded believers who adhere to the exalted Christ and sound theology. These house churches are typical worldwide, though not as much in America.

They are not out-of-line with the early church and could be an option for those hungering for God's Word and koinonia. Of course, there is your family. If all you have are the folks in your household, do not neglect to gather for teaching, praying, singing, and administering the Word within your family. The Bible would assume that the authority figure in the home would do this regardless of church options, but sometimes, it's the only option. As we saw during the pandemic, the suicide rate and psychological complications spiked because folks isolated from each other. Isolation is one of the worst forms of punishment, and no Christian should crave it over the community, no matter how small that community may be.

Call to Action

1. Define the gospel from an ontological and orthopraxy perspective.
2. Why is the gospel of first importance in a church? In what ways could a church be off regarding the gospel? What would happen if the church's view of the gospel was off?
3. Why would a skewed view of the gospel corrupt a church's understanding of theology? What are some examples of messed-up theology because of a wrong understanding of the gospel? E.g., social gospel.
4. Let's say the church has some of the best ministries you've ever experienced, but their theology was heretical. Why would it be dangerous for you and your family to continue in that church?
5. What are some reasons folks would retreat from the church? How would you steelman your arguments, making a case that it's okay not to attend a church?
6. Collect all the "one another" verses in the New Testament for an extended project and choose a few to apply to your life. What did you learn? What were the applications? How do you think this exercise will change you?
7. After you make a few applications, speak with someone about this project, sharing what God did in your heart and life through this exercise.

5

Three Fantastic Characteristics

The best local churches have values distinct from the culture, while transforming the church's community to reach the culture with the gospel to export those values to the next generation. When looking for a fantastic local church, there are many things to consider, in addition to their views on the gospel and sound theology. What are a few things that come to your mind? Let me share with you three characteristics that all local churches should prioritize.

Decorating the House

All roads in your local church flow from the gospel—the person and work of Jesus Christ. If the gospel is not of first importance in your church, everything else will prove ineffective (1 Corinthians 15:3), making your church search a non-starter. Think about the church like a house. A home has a foundation; that's the gospel. There is a structure that sits on that foundation. In this illustration, the structure is sound theology. With the foundation set and the structure assembled, you can now decorate the house with the amenities.

Perhaps you have recognized houses with weak

foundations (gospel). Maybe you've seen poorly constructed homes (theology). I have. If the foundation is unstable and the structure is not sound, the rest of the house will not compensate for those two blunders. The proper foundation is why the gospel is the most significant value you want in any church. Because this is not an either-or proposition, sound theology is the second most critical value. If you're satisfied with your church's focus and implementation of a practical gospel by sound theology, you can move on to the following three essentials of a fantastically, effective church.

- Worship
- Ministries
- Fellowship

A local church's worship value is not primarily about the music but the lifestyle because you never ask, "Are you worshiping?" The reason is that we worship all the time. God made us for worship—wired us for worship, you could say. Worship is part of what it means to be image-bearers. Who could do otherwise? The better question is, "What or whom do we worship?" We won't have to think too deeply about this because there are only two answers: we are worshiping God or ourselves—however this latter option plays out differently in our practical lives.

Evaluating Worship

Worship communicates who we are as people—our state of being, and what we do—our behaviors. Worship needs a source (heart) that motivates the worshiper's actions. It's the actions that reveal the worshiper's heart (Matthew 7:16; Luke 6:45). For the Christian, the source of worship is the gospel (Christ), and the object of worship is the gospel (Christ). Jesus is the why and the what of worship. Any other source or object of worship is idolatry, making Christian worship distinctly Christ-centered.

A gospel-centered local church provides a context for God's people to break away from earthly tethering so they can freely worship according to their identity. Local church gatherings give Christians a place that foreshadows what Christians of all ages will do in eternity—worship Christ. Though there is much to do to put on a church meeting and a lot of activities at a church meeting, one primary point for all this activity is to create an ease of focus for the worshiper to adore and enjoy God. Here are a few questions that will help you examine the worship experience at your church.

- How do your friends motivate you to worship the Savior?
- How does the music lead you to engage the Savior?
- How would you rate your anticipation during the week to worship Christ at your local church meetings?
- Is your church meeting a God-centered worship event that refreshes your soul?

Music Note: Because worship is our lives, our church's music style is a preferential, tertiary matter. The lyrics, on the other hand, are of first importance. Lyrics, like preaching, must find their grounding in the gospel because they proclaim what is essential to God (Mark 1:11).

Evaluating Ministries

An essential part of any local church is the ministries of that church. Paul exhorts pastors to equip the saints to do the work of the ministry (Ephesians 4:11–14). He further urges leaders to help the people under their care to become mature in their faith. Solid, thought-out ministries provide a context for Christians to grow in Christ. Ministries are one of the better things a local church can provide for its people. Gospel-centered ministries point the people to Jesus. They are a means of grace that lead people to a greater understanding and practice of Christ. The best ministries are transformative.

Ministry Downsides

MINISTRY SUBSTITUTES: Ministries should never replace the activities in the home. Ministries are not surrogate parents. Christian parents do not give up their responsibilities as parents to any ministry, program, or local church. Parents parent children. Parents determine the means of grace (ministries) necessary to facilitate Christian maturity. Church ministries are supplemental resources that accomplish parental goals. Ministries are not parental replacements. Ministries do not interfere with or circumvent parental responsibilities. The local church does not do our jobs as parents, and they should not interfere with our responsibilities. Gospel-centered ministries make our jobs as parents better.

MINISTRY SLAVERY: As much as I love our church building, I do not plan to live there. You should not either. It's just a building; that's all. Guard your time and your calendar against being ministry-centered. For some Christians, there is a temptation to be ministry-centered. Their lives revolve around what they do for their local churches. Ministry slavery is dangerous. Christians revolve around the gospel while the local church ministries ensure that gospel-centered worldview.

MINISTRY PREFERENCES: Ministries are the niceties of religion, which is a plus. But if I lived where it was impossible to have what we have in our local church, I'm confident God's grace would be sufficient, and we would be okay. Guard against elevating the importance of a church ministry as though the lives of your family depend on it. A biblical family with few church ministries is far better than an unbiblical family that expects the church to meet all their preferences.

- How do the ministries of your church supplement your Christian life?
- Are you ministry-centered, family-centered, or friend-centered—if these were your three choices?
- Have you over-elevated the importance of ministries?
- How are you making the ministries of your local church more effective?

Fellowship

"I visited that church, and no one shook my hand." Have you ever heard that complaint? Have you ever grumbled that way? The idea of the unfriendly church is one of the most misunderstood aspects of any local congregation. Not being friendly or not connecting with others is expected because it's part of the Adamic curse. People come into the world wrapped in guilt and shame, a temptation that motivates us to resist transparency, isolating ourselves from God and the community. Even friendly people struggle with transparency. People are not predisposed to love you the way you want to experience love and kindness. If you remember this thought, you won't be disappointed when you look for transparent people to build a community in your local church. A lack of interactive connectivity is not as much a church problem as an Adam problem.

No matter what local church you attend, you will find it challenging to locate a context where people are willing to be humble, open, transparent, honest, vulnerable, and self-disclosing about their lives with you. Fellowship or community (koinonia) is a Spirit-led, humble, transparent, reciprocal community that focuses on what God is doing in the participants' lives. My appeal to you is not to sit around waiting for someone to engage you the way you want engagement. A gospel-centered church does not sit around waiting on a handshake or complain about not connecting with others. Christ did not sit in heaven demanding us to come to Him. He took on the form of a servant and came to us to help us become what we are supposed to be (Philippians 2:7). Rather than sitting, soaking, and expecting others to pursue us, it would be better for us to become the pursuers.

- True community is not a passive activity.
- True community is not for the timid.
- True community requires spiritual aggression.

Sadly, some people come from backgrounds where honesty, openness, and vulnerability are not valued. Honesty led to harsh judgments. They have not lived in gospel-motivated contexts and are tempted to be distant and cynical. These dangerous side-effects of religion and authoritative constructs are why a gospel-centered local church is essential. Your interpretative grid for fellowship (community) will have flaws if you don't have the gospel right. Your temptation will be self-protection, not self-disclosure. If your church is not self-disclosing, be patient. It takes years for people to become comfortable enough to let you into the real world of their thought lives. Don't make your passion for transparency a mandate for the tentative Christian. Milton Vincent gives the perfect antidote to overcome the fear of what others may think or say about you.

If I wanted others to think highly of me, I would conceal the fact that a shameful slaughter of the perfect son of God was required so that I might be saved. But when I stand at the foot of the Cross and am seen by others under the light of that Cross, I am left uncomfortably exposed before their eyes. Indeed, the most humiliating gossip that could ever be whispered about me is blared from Golgotha's hill; and my self-righteous reputation is left in ruins in the wake of its revelations. With the worst facts about me thus exposed to the view of others, I find myself feeling that I truly have nothing left to hide. —The Gospel Primer, by Milton Vincent

Building Community

- You begin by being honest with God. You reveal to Him what He already knows about you (Hebrews 4:13).
- You let your spouse (or close friend) into your secret world of shame, hurt, pain, victory, praise, and grace—incrementally and appropriately.
- You search for like-minded believers within your congregation who want to go to this level with you.

Ask God to lead you to this kind of person. Then, start sharing yourself while drawing out what is in their hearts. Your goal is to build a group of transparent friends. If you are married, your community begins with your spouse and then your children. Don't assume others will have your vision for or your understanding of true biblical fellowship. Some Christians have not experienced gospel-based relationships. Guard your heart against self-righteously judging others unwilling to pursue this with you. There are reasons why they are reluctant. See if they will let you help them. By all means, lead by example. If you want this kind of community, you must make it happen. It will not happen on its own. Do not be that guy in the back row, expecting someone to shake his hand.

Imagine a church that understands and practically practices the gospel. Their theology is precise, and they communicate it. The people exemplify a lifestyle of worship every day. The church provides ministries that supplement who the people are and engage each other in an authentic, self-disclosing community. That is a beautiful body. I suspect your church is not that yet. That's okay. It's more about direction than perfection. Are they heading in the right direction? Are you helping them get there? You are not looking for the perfect church. You're looking for a church moving in the right direction, which you measure by their ongoing and practical implementation of the gospel in their lives.

Call to Action

1. Describe worship, which is more than music. How does your life represent a robust worshiping Christian? What area do you need to address and change?
2. How would you speak with a person with a narrow view of worship? He's looking for a church but defines worship as the singers and their songs. Though this criterion is vital, why would you want him to broaden his assessment of the church regarding worship?
3. What ministries would you like to have in your church?
4. What ministry do you believe is the best fit for you?
5. Have you ever fallen for any of the three ministry downsides? If you have, what was the process to overcome them? What is your plan to change if you perceive them as traps in your life today?
6. How would you disciple the grumbler who talks about the unfriendly church? Why do folks tend to isolate and build cliques versus having a gospel-centered, gospel-going worldview?
7. What is the solution for the grumbler? How will you motivate this person to actively seek friends rather than passively complain about not having friends?

6

Qualities of a Pastor

One of the most important questions when looking for a new church is how the pastor leads the local church. In larger churches, it's a unified body of pastors. It would be an excellent thought experiment to answer a few questions about those who lead your church. What best describes your pastor? How does he affect those around him? Can he care for your soul? Finding a good shepherd is a tedious process that can even be daunting. Ensuring the proper leader leads the community well is paramount because he determines everything that flows from that local body.

Which Shepherd?

We are looking for a new church. Would you mind answering this question for us: If you were looking for a church, what kind of pastor would you be looking for in that church? I know many things to consider when hunting for a church, but we wondered about leadership and what makes a good pastor. Thanks for your time.

—Supporting Member

> I am the good shepherd. The good shepherd lays down his life for the sheep.
>
> (John 10:11)

The first step is to seek advice. It is wise, humble, and essential because another set of eyes will reveal things you did not consider, and the decision is too big to make without external input. Church life is one of your life's three most significant spheres with work and family comprising the other two. We live most of our lives in these interrelated circles, and when any one of them becomes unsettled, it can make life uncertain and even uncomfortable.

When I think about the church question, my primary thought is, "Who do I want to be my shepherd?" I like to frame the church question this way, especially when you substitute the word pastor for the word shepherd. Jesus called Himself the Good Shepherd, and that speaks volumes about the kind of person He was and the kind of person we need to come alongside us as we lead our lives and families. He needs to be a competent, caring soul with all the courage necessary to help us mature into Christlikeness. He won't be perfect as Jesus was, but he will be objectively developing into Christlikeness.

Under-shepherds

> He makes me lie down in green pastures. He leads me beside still waters. He restores my soul. He leads me in paths of righteousness for his name's sake.
>
> (Psalm 23:2-3)

We automatically connect the word shepherd to the kind of people we are: sheep. While sheep are not typically a flattering term, it is an accurate one. You cannot trust sheep to meander down the trails of life without the expert care of a good shepherd. The Lord knew this, which is why He gave the church under-shepherds to care for His sheep. Under-shepherds help us do things that are not spiritually intuitive to us. I am not calling you foolish—at least you are not more foolish than I am. But you must receive care from others, which is one of the many things that distinguishes Christians from our worldly counterparts.

We humbly recognize our need to receive care while seeking interdependent relationships, and none of those outside relationships are more critical than the shepherd we want to submit to receive his care. Shepherding care does not mean the church's lead pastor or the team will be personally pastoring us. That is not always possible, especially if you land in a large church. Of course, the size of the church should not matter. Congregational size is a matter of personal preference. You can receive the pastor's care regardless of the size, though not always his undivided attention. Paul provided insight on how to care for folks without giving every single person face time.

Caring for People

> *To equip the saints for the work of ministry, for building up the body of Christ, until we all attain the unity of the faith and of the knowledge of the Son of God, to mature manhood, to the measure of the stature of the fullness of Christ, so that we may no longer be children, tossed to and fro by the waves and carried about by every wind of doctrine, by human cunning, by craftiness in deceitful schemes.*
> (Ephesians 4:12–14)

The shepherd's role is not what he does for you but what he provides for you. Though the pastor may not give you his undivided attention, he can offer you expert care. The kind of care he provides for you and others will flow out of the type of person he is and into his immediate sphere that does receive his undivided attention—other leaders in the church. The pastor of a small church and a large church are the same in that they determine the shepherding care the church provides and the sheep receive. Regardless of the church's size, the church leaders set the attitude, direction, and quality of the care.

A lead pastor's primary role is to lead by caring for you individually or leading those who are caring for you. If the church has a lot of people, the pastor will equip others to care for you. These individuals will carry out his shepherding vision and direction for the church. Suppose he is a pastor of a smaller congregation. In that case, he may be doing the primary soul care for the congregation while identifying a few core people to come alongside himself to help in the shepherding responsibilities. Either way, the sheep who are part of the local church he leads should be receiving his world-class shepherding care.

World-class Care

The LORD is my shepherd; I shall not want
(Psalm 23:1)

No doubt the shepherd you find will be wearing many hats, but the main one you want to discern is his soul-care hat. With all charity and discernment, you must ask, what is the condition or state of the sheep under his care? How are they doing? If you were to go to an auction where they were selling sheep, you would want to know the health of the sheep. The quality of the sheep will directly reflect the kind of shepherd who was in charge of caring for them. The quality of care is such an essential point that our Good Shepherd will judge His under-shepherds. Of course, I'm not talking about those rogue sheep who sporadically wander into the fold or have a low commitment to the church.

> Obey your leaders and submit to them, for they are keeping watch over your souls, as those who will have to give an account. Let them do this with joy and not with groaning, for that would be of no advantage to you.
>
> (Hebrews 13:17)

The Hebrew text is a fearful passage that should motivate pastors to care for their people competently and diligently. Though I am not a pastor, and God will not judge me the same way as a pastor (James 3:1), this verse is a sober reminder of the seriousness of a person's shepherding responsibilities. We must also not miss the caveat: we must let our pastors pastor us with joy, not groaning. As you assess your pastor, evaluate yourself: Are you a joy for him to pastor? Perhaps asking him would be an opportunity for you to conversate about the reciprocality of partnering with your pastor.

A Pastor's Family

> So I exhort the elders among you, as a fellow elder and a witness of the sufferings of Christ, as well as a partaker in the glory that is going to be revealed: shepherd the flock of God that is among you, exercising oversight, not under compulsion, but willingly, as God would have you; not for shameful gain, but eagerly; not domineering over those in your charge, but being examples to the flock.
>
> (1 Peter 5:1–3)

Peter considered the elders to be examples to the flock, another fundamental perspective you look for in a good shepherd. What kind of example is the pastor of the church you are considering? There are ways for you to discern the exemplary care-competence of your potential under-shepherd; it's his impact on others, including carefully considering his wife and children, assuming he has a wife and kids. His family will provide you with the most accurate assessment of the kind of person he has been.

- What has been his effect on others? How has he affected those closest to the epicenter of his sphere of influence?
- How would you describe his wife?
- Does she give you the impression that she has received excellent shepherding care from her husband? The longer the marriage, the more she has been affected by him.
- What is her sanctification trajectory? Is she maturing more and more into Christlikeness?

Though she is personally responsible for how she grows in Christ, there is no question that her shepherd husband has affected her. You cannot live close to another human being for an extended period and not affect that person, whether for the good or bad. What about his children? What are they like? How do they carry themselves, interact with others, and engage in life if they are in their upper teens or beyond? These things will reflect how the primary influencer in their lives has influenced them. Their dad is the one who has had the most powerful impact on their lives. As you observe his children, what kind of vibe do you pick up from them?

I am not asking you the regeneration or passion for Christ questions. If they have been born again or are passionate for the Lord, that is between them and the Lord. None of us can insert salvation or passion into our children because those functions fall within the sphere of grace rather than the works of men. What you are looking for is how their dad has shaped their personalities. You are not looking for perfection in any of these qualities but rather the presence of Christlike shepherding from their dad. Similar to his wife, what has been his imprint on his children? No sheep exhibits perfection. We all have flaws, but a discernible element of care has affected the person.

- Do they struggle with the fear of man?
- Are they sociable?
- Are they mature in how they engage in life?
- Do they know how to behave appropriately among their peers?

Shepherding Question

You prepare a table before me in the presence of my enemies.

(Psalm 23:5)

These observations are essential because you are not just asking the shepherding question for yourself. Your responsibilities before God are more significant than your unique sanctification aspirations. God has called you to lead your family, which means, in part, making sure you position them to receive the best possible soul care from the various ways the Lord provides. When I think about the local church I attend, one of the questions I ask, which is related to the shepherding question, goes like this:

> If I were to die, has my pastor created a culture in our church that would be a safe and nurturing environment for my wife and children to continue to grow in their sanctification? Will my wife and children be safely cared for while helped to fend off the enemies of their souls?

Psalm 23:5 makes the shepherding question much more extensive than who will care for you in the here and now. Who do you want to bring long-term, futuristic care to your wife and children should you die? When you decide on the church where you will plant your family, you will be placing them under the care of a shepherd who will have a present and future impact on their souls.

Soul Care Expert

> He must not be a recent convert, or he may become puffed up with conceit and fall into the condemnation of the devil.
>
> (1 Timothy 3:6)

Your decision has long-term consequences. Another way I like to think about this question is similar to how I reflect on a surgeon. Let's say you were going under the knife, or maybe your wife was going under the knife. What kind of person do you want to do surgery on you? How about your wife? Who do you trust to do this? Surgery is not a rash decision as you can see. You are looking for a person who is competent enough to provide the shepherding care and contexts that Jesus wants your wife and children to have. The shepherding question is one of the most important questions you can ask when looking for a church.

Though the shepherd may know how to preach and lead an organization, his application and practice of soul care will significantly impact you and your family. Paul did not preach in the most appealing or expected ways, but he knew how to care for souls (1 Corinthians 2:1–5). A great orator for a pastor may be a plus, but it is not a must. Even being a world-class CEO who knows how to run a world-class organization is not bad, but his ability to provide personal soul care and soul care contexts will be of utmost importance.

Call to Action

1. Can your pastor shepherd you? Can he provide shepherding contexts for you? Please explain your answer.
2. Can he speak into your life and your spouse's life in such a way that changes you and your spouse? How do you know?
3. Can you and your family mature in Christ while under his leadership? Will your spouse and children grow in Christ after you leave?

Qualities of a Pastor

7

Signs of Spiritual Abuse

A supporting member asked, "Can you give some clear examples of signs of how a pastor or church leader is crossing the line from being a shepherd to a spiritual abuser? It would be helpful to know when to support a pastor when he is genuinely trying to defend and protect his flock from outside and wrong influence vs. a pastor who has an agenda and is above questioning or accountability. The lines sometimes seem blurred, and I would appreciate your help distinguishing these differences."

Internal Disordering

What you're calling spiritual abuse happens when someone is determined to evilly manipulate another person to accomplish an ungodly agenda. Anytime anyone sins against another person, including physical and sexual harm, it is spiritual abuse—or the disordering of one's soul. You cannot physically or sexually harm someone without adversely affecting their inner being—their spiritual selves. I realize the question is not asking about physical or sexual abuse but rather is asking a question about the internal adverse impact on one's soul, which is what all sin does.

Humans are two parts—dichotomy: physical and

spiritual. The spiritual aspects of a person include the soul, spirit, mind, will, emotions, thoughts, intentions, etc. The physical also has several parts, e.g., internal organs and external body parts. Spiritual abuse happens to the soul, which primarily affects the mind—how a person thinks, and you'll see emotional manifestations from their thought processes. Spiritual disordering takes the victim's thoughts captive by trying to manipulate them into believing lies. Suppose the internal disordering of the soul continues unabated because of the antagonist's sin. In that case, it will exponentially affect the person spiritually, especially how they relate to God and others.

Darkness comes over their souls, leading to depression, despair, despondency, and even suicide. It also leads to erratic behaviors like random anger, fear-motivated withdrawal, or alleviating mechanisms like alcohol and medications. Alleviating happens to someone more than you may think, which makes the question relevant. The most common place where you find spiritual abuse is in contexts where someone has authority over someone else, whether the power is God-given or self-proclaimed.

Home and Church

Bad marriages and horrible churches are two of your typical breeding grounds for this type of sinful activity perpetrated on the vulnerable. It can also occur in work environments. In these contexts, there are God-given hierarchies. These biblical structures will become dangerous when the sinful person wants to dominate someone. God pre-wired people to follow and submit to others. Paul called Christians to follow other Christians (Ephesians 5:1; 1 Corinthians 11:1; Philippians 4:8). Our culture calls this the herd mentality, which is an unfortunate connotation.

Christians call it biblical wisdom and humility to submit and follow. The world does not function well without hierarchal structures as we see in our current equal outcome culture where everyone is on the same level functionally and should receive equal outcomes. God did not wire us to be independent gods but to follow Him and others, making a hierarchy crucial for our well-being. You see this notion throughout the Old and New Testaments. God elevated leaders for His people to follow. So far, so good. The problem comes when some leaders forget their God-given call and God-illuminated directives for leading others well.

> Not many of you should become teachers, my brothers, for you know that we who teach will be judged with greater strictness
>
> (James 3:1)

Proceed with Caution

However, this question is a dangerous one. It is dangerous because it can unsettle and even destroy a local church. I appreciate the carefulness and sobriety with which the questioner approached this subject. There are souls at stake. If there is no spiritual abuse, discretion is paramount so that our Christian brothers and sisters are not discouraged by the discourse. If there is spiritual abuse, caution is crucial because our Christian brothers and sisters are in harm's way. They need help; you must warn them, and intervention must happen.

The other people group you want to think about are those who reject our religion. You do not want to give them more ammunition for their already well-stocked arsenals. The most significant concern is God's fame, of course. You want to make God's name great in all you do, so you cannot ignore potential spiritual abuse, especially when you are made aware that it is happening. To be silent about the abuse makes you culpable in a less consequential way.

Signs of Spiritual Abuse

I appreciate our questioner's love for humanity and the body of Christ. I admire his courage because he is willing to speak up on a far more critical matter than some of the things we like to turn into arguments. To answer the question, I'm going to ask you eight questions. It would be foolish for me to pretend that I know the answer to his question when I don't know what is happening. However, I do understand the problem and will provide you with eight signs of spiritual abuse. I trust these responses will help you to determine what might be happening in your situation. My questions do not represent an exhaustive list or a list in order of importance.

Eight Signs of Possible Abuse

1: Do You Have to Ask?

If you have to ask whether a person is spiritually abusive, that may be your first sign. Think about Jesus here. Nobody asked that question about Him—nobody with any common sense. If you are sitting under a pastor and you have a general sense of uneasiness about him, you need to explore this—first:

1. Start with your thoughts.
2. Then, with God.
3. With your spouse, if you're married.
4. Possibly a close confidant.
5. Please keep a tight net around your thoughts, at least initially. It will become apparent to all if you are right, but if you are not, you do not want to mischaracterize a person's reputation or discourage others unnecessarily.

2: Does He Delegate?

Abusive pastors are usually controllers. They like to micromanage their organization and their people. There is one way to do things, and it is their way. Alternatively, when abuse is not there, you will find much biblical liberty that taps into the diversity in Christ's body. The controller does not appreciate opinions; they are not encouraged or celebrated.

3: Does He Clone Leaders?

Along with his tight control over how the church operates, you will also sense that he only uses those in lockstep with him. Think Hitler here. Hitler believed in a superior way and granted promotion only to those who gave allegiance to him. You had to have his trust to carry out his policies using his methods. The spiritual abuser will test his candidates, usually with extra-biblical guidelines—his guidelines. The people promoted within his system will think and act similarly to him. They are pawns who won't buck the system—his system. One of the instructive things you'll find with his underlings is that if you ask them a question they do not know the answer to, they will not be able to provide an answer. They will have to check with HQ first. The Spirit of God and His Word are no longer leading the church. The leaders keep in step with another kind of spirit.

4: Does He Clone a Culture?

Because of his heavy-handed control and his cloning of leaders, you will begin to notice a lack of diversity in your church. They will create their language, mannerisms, and customs like the leader. When guests visit, they will notice how different it is from other local churches. Those inside the clone factory will take this as a compliment. Those outside the clone factory will think it is a cult. No sensible Christian should walk into any Christian church and believe it is a cult because of its unique language, mannerisms, or customs.

Paul wrote to many churches, teaching them how to think and behave, and you see a consistent pattern throughout church history of local church body life. Within diversity in all the local churches, there is a similarity between those churches worldwide. If your church is becoming something other than what anyone would typically expect from a New Testament, local church—while making allowances for pneumatic (Spirit-led) diversity—there may be a danger. This problem will point back to the tight-fisted control of the leader.

5: How Do You Think?

If you are not around your pastor, are you less guarded? Are you free to be you? I am not talking about the fear of pastor syndrome, where insecure people are intimidated by authority figures or people who overly exalt their pastor, thinking he is bigger than life. One of the pastor's greatest strengths is his ability to build up another person while humanizing himself. Do you feel edified and free to be the person God calls you to be, or are you more cautious about your words and actions around him? Think about Hitler again.

If I were around Hitler, I would guard my words and actions. If I were around Jesus, I would be relaxed and free to be myself. If I were not relaxed, He would lead me into that freedom (Psalm 23:1–6). I know I can make a mistake around Jesus. I would be nervous about messing up around Hitler. The abusive pastor makes you more self-aware and self-conscious. You feel more constricted and less free, especially when around him.

6: Are You Free to Speak?

Can you tell him what you are thinking? Let's go back to Jesus again. Prayer is one of your most beautiful means of grace as God's child. You are encouraged to talk to Him. You can tell Him anything and never fear undesirable repercussions. Your pastor is the Lord's under-shepherd. God called him to emulate the Savior as he provides an example for you to follow. You should be as free to talk to your pastor as you are free to speak to the Lord.

> Not domineering over those in your charge, but being examples to the flock.
>
> (1 Peter 5:3)

- Can you share your concerns with him, whatever they are?
- Do you believe you can trust him?
- Does your pastor steward your thoughts and concerns like Jesus, always seeking your best?
- Can you disagree with him?
- Does he approach your differing opinions as a learner, not a defender of his position?
- Is he willing to allow you to exercise your views as long as they are not contrary to the Bible?
- Is he willing to change his mind because he sees the wisdom and value from your input?

7: Is He Ignorant?

> He must not be a recent convert, or he may become puffed up with conceit.
>
> (1 Timothy 3:6)

A pastor can be a novice. He may not be a recent convert, but he could act like one. One of the patterns I have noticed in our church culture today is how the process for selecting pastors does not pay attention to the more essential details. In many cases, the qualifications for a pastor are not 1 Timothy 3:1-7. It is more about a person's ambition to be in a ministry—possibly his education, charisma, and leadership ability. The church is looking for a particular guy, but his character is not at the top of the list.

A genuine desire to be a pastor and an excellent pastoral education or a leadership gift does not make you a good leader. Hitler had two of these: a strong desire to be great and a pronounced leadership gift, though twisted. He was not an educated man, but he was street-smart. The qualifications Paul gave Timothy were mostly about a person's character. Except for the gift of teaching, the criteria for a pastor are the same for any believer. They are Christlike character traits found in the person's heart, which take much time to discern.

There have been too many instances where folks have given men the reins of a local church, even though they were deficient in character. Premature promotion is a disaster for the church people, the pastor, his family, and God's fame. It is easier not to put a person in ministry than to put him in ministry and remove him later. The fallout can be disastrous and generational.

8: Is He Humble?

Has he created an environment for personal growth and relationship building? Servant leaders develop environments of grace where those they serve can grow and mature into the unique Christlike people God called them to be. The humility of the leader accomplishes this, not his pride. The spiritual abuse question also applies to us: can our spouses and our friends share their concerns with us, whatever they may be? If they cannot share because of our immaturity, anger, or unwillingness to listen, we must reconsider how we may affect them. A humble man or woman will want to hear about areas of weakness because he's never about himself. The humble pastor welcomes grace-motivated, grace-concerned individuals seeking his best for God's glory. That kind of pastor is an active learner willing to change, grow, and mature. He's a good under-shepherd.

Call to Action

1. Is there an authority figure in your life whom you believe is abusing you, or someone else? How do they align with these eight signs? Perhaps you can add other potential signs.
2. If you believe abuse is happening, will you talk to a competent and trusted friend about this to affirm or dismiss your assumptions? It's not wrong to talk to others about someone else if your motives are redemptive and you hope to resolve a potential issue.

8

Preaching or Discipleship

The preaching of God's Word is essential for life transformation, but preaching alone is not enough to change lives and families. A transformational church is both a preaching center and a discipleship community. A preaching center and discipleship community work in tandem from the pulpit to the living room. With sound, theological wisdom flowing from the pulpit, the church is in a position to disseminate and distill the preached Word in applicable and practical ways throughout the week so that the church member can experience transformation.

An Unraveling Marriage

Mable has been a Christian for twenty-three years. She attended a Christian college and received a degree in business administration. She met Biff in her junior year; they married and had two children, Biffy and Biffina. Mable is young and intelligent. She loves God and is courageous in her faith. She is humble and seeks to please God as she walks out her faith. Biff once had a similar passion for God, which was the main thing that drew Mable to him during their college days.

As the years passed, Biff became more interested in

his work than his wife. He works twelve to fourteen-hour days during the week. On the weekends, Biff goes into his hibernation-vegetative mode, as Mable calls it; he consumes an endless selection from ESPN. He also seems depressed around the house while at other times he has fits of anger, which seem to have no cause.

Their marriage is unraveling as the love they once had for each other is getting lost in the maze of a frustrating life. Mable approached one of the elders at her church regarding the inevitable conjugal collapse. He could only direct her to a book on meeting one another's needs that his wife had recently read. His other counsel was just as hopeless in that it provided little direction.

The Great Preacher

After months of long-suffering and idea exhaustion, Mable came to me with the problems of her marriage. I attempted to direct her back to her local church, but she related her futile attempts at getting help with words of cynicism. I asked her why she attended her church, and she gave me a line I had often heard in my counseling relationships: "I love the preaching at my church." I felt the tension building in my body as I compared her response to the seemingly inevitable collapse of her marriage.

Biblical counselors have many counseling dilemmas and tensions as they interact with people with problems. One common difficulty is the question I posed to Mable: "Why do you attend your church?" Typically, the answer is similar to the one Mable gave: "I love my church because the teaching is outstanding. The pastor is an excellent expositor." And I have heard responses like, "The preaching is so good. Our pastor holds our attention with great stories and is so down to earth. He's relevant."

These answers may be accurate descriptors of a good preacher and sound preaching, and I would say (and hope) that all our teachers of the Word are so gifted in their oratory skill and exegetical precision. I never want to minimize the gift needed to proclaim God's Word; it is a gift, and not everyone who desires the noble task of teaching has the skill or, as Paul would say, the "ability to teach." This blessed ability to teach comes with the critical office of a pastor. If a man does not have the aptitude to teach, it is certain that God did not call him to a full-time vocational teaching ministry, as Paul lays out for us in 1 Timothy 3:1–7.

The Great System

I never want to minimize the need for gifting, exposition, skill, relevance, and excellent illustrations to bring clarity to God's Word as one presents it to a congregation during a church meeting. However, we need to think through our methodology for how we disseminate and customize the Word of God into the individual lives of the congregation after the preaching event. To Mable, I want to say, "If the preaching is that great, which I do not doubt, how come you have so many unresolved problems?"

As a counselor, I'm filtering Mable's answer about her church through the lens of the life and marriage I'm counseling. What would the great Apostle to the Gentiles say regarding his "great" preaching? Could it be a robust Christian faith requires something more than great preaching? Could American Christianity have placed an unguarded emphasis on preaching, exposition, word studies, oratory skill, and cultural relevance? Listen to Paul.

> And I, when I came to you, brothers, did not come proclaiming to you the testimony of God with lofty speech or wisdom. For I decided to know nothing among you except Jesus Christ and him crucified. And I was with you in weakness and in fear and much trembling, and my speech and my message were not

in plausible words of wisdom, but in demonstration of the Spirit and of power, so that your faith might not rest in the wisdom of men but in the power of God.

(1 Corinthians 2:1–5)

Teaching Plus Training

As John Piper reflects on these verses, he writes,

> In other words, (Paul) avoided the ostentation of oratory and intellect. Why? What was the ground of this demeanor in preaching? Verse 2 tells us very plainly: "For I decided to know nothing among you except Jesus Christ and him crucified." I think what he means by this verse is that he set his mind to be so saturated with the crucifying power of the cross that in everything he said and did, in all his preaching, there would be the aroma of death—death to self-reliance, death to pride, death to boasting in man—so that the life that people would see would be the life of Christ, and the power that people would see would be the power of God. Why?
>
> Why did he want people to see this and not himself? Verse 5 answers: "So that your faith might not rest in the wisdom of men but in the power of God." In other words, that God (not the preacher!) might be honored in the trust of his people. That's the goal of preaching![1]

I would take Piper's thought and push it further by suggesting that there must be a methodology for sanctification that takes the powerfully preached Word of God that exalts Jesus Christ and works it out through the fabric of the individual lives that make up the local church.

---

1 John Piper *The Supremacy of God in Preaching*, Grand Rapids: Baker Books, 1990, 38.

Without a system for Christians to grow, preaching the Word can lose its intended effect on the local church. The result of the preached Word can become forgotten by the time the listener exits the building on any given Sunday.

We see in Paul's letters to the churches a system, as he lays out in those letters a methodology on how to live the Christian life in the context of the community. Paul's method goes from the pulpit—the Christ-exalting teaching he provided, to the community where Christian living takes place. One way to see Paul's plan for community application of the Word is to study the "one another" sayings in his writings. Paul created a community effect for Christian growth. Remember, Paul's preaching was not a series of stand-alone events with no follow-up. His letters, full of "one another" verses, were the explanations and practical outworking of his preaching.

The Center and Community

Paul preached the Word, and he carefully unpacked the Word for personal application through his writings. Paul's letters were his God-inspired and God-ordained methodology for progressive and consistent growth for the Christian. This "power of God" that Piper talks about is often not worked out (Philippians 2:12–14) and applied to the average church member through a crucified life.

It's not unusual for a typical Christian to be blind to God's comprehensive approach to sanctification that extends from the pulpit to the living room. American Christianity, in part, seems to have concluded that the key to the success of the local church is tied almost exclusively to the man in the pulpit. This success is proportionate to his ability to relate to the average person on Sunday morning.

The outcome of this kind of thinking can lead people to create a preaching center rather than a discipleship community. You can quickly identify the preaching center because it's a church that progressively weakens as you move from the pulpit to the periphery. Power and relevance in the pulpit, which could very well be true, does not mean the congregants are necessarily growing in their personal and progressive sanctification.

Relational Disconnectedness

These same congregants may be accumulating Bible knowledge and worldview awareness. Still, all too often, they are relationally disconnected from their local church body and have very little substantive and direct accountability that impacts their lives in practical, relevant, and biblical ways. They come to their counseling sessions raving about the powerful preaching they hear weekly. Still, they often cannot see that their practical, functional Christianity does not demonstrate the power of God through daily living.

There is no real plan for the present, future, and ongoing change; still, the people love their church because of the great preaching. The preaching, seemingly, has the same effect as reading the daily news or watching a documentary; they hear it, think about it, and may even tell a friend about it, but the Word does not transform them. They grow in Bible trivia but are not progressively changing daily, week-to-week, or year-to-year. Could some people be substituting great pulpit speaking for their responsibility for meaningful, long-term, and personal sanctification?

Could it be that their views of personal sanctification are truncated at the pulpit rather than extended into their daily lives? Do they think the pulpit is the beginning and the end of God's methodology for sound sanctification—for Christian maturity? If preaching, defined as a monologue from the pulpit to the pew, is so important, why did Jesus rarely use this method of communication? Though God has commanded preaching His gospel, growth in gospel grace requires much more than sitting and soaking.

Monologue or Dialogue?

Note what author, lecturer, and counselor David Powlison says on this point.

> Several years ago, I happened to be reading the gospel of Mark while thinking about these matters. So, I took apart five chapters (Mark 7–11), looking not for the content of Jesus' teaching, but for the context in which his ministry of the gospel took place. I asked, "Is what happens in this scene one-way preaching or two-way conversation?" These observations are not normative in any way ("You must have the same ratio of interpersonal ministry to public ministry as Jesus has." "You should quote Scripture as often—or as infrequently—as Jesus.") No, we are only watching and describing.
>
> I mean this to be provocative and illustrational. These five chapters contain 26 scenes. Jesus talks in every scene, but four scenes are predominantly action. Here Jesus lives his message. In these incidents, he ministers the Word and proclaims the gospel by incarnating the message, arousing faith by actions. The verbal exchanges that take place are directives related to his actions. The other 22 scenes contain verbal ministry of the Word. How many portray public proclamation to the crowd? How many capture the back and forth of interpersonal conversation?
>
> There are four instances of public ministry, of sermons to crowds. Only one of these (8:34–9:1) did not either arise from an earlier conversation or lead to a subsequent conversation. That leaves eighteen scenes in which Jesus does the interpersonal ministry of the Word. Striking, isn't it? Jesus converses the Word. Is that part of your associations

to the ministry of the Word? He interacts with the gospel. Does that come to mind when you think 'proclamation of the gospel'? No surprise, whether Jesus is preaching or counseling, he always puts things in a way that meets people.

He engages their questions, reactions, thoughts, experiences, concerns, troubles, motives, blind spots, circumstances, hopes. If you extract Matthew 5–7, you would find little public ministry of the Word in comparison to the private ministry of the Word. Jesus' main method of communicating his truth was a two-way dialogue, not a one-way monologue. He lived in the contexts of his people and interacted with them primarily. [2]

Call to Action

1. Why do you attend your church?
2. Is your church a preaching center and a discipleship community? Is its strength in one or the other?
3. List how your church practicalizes the gospel in the people's everyday lives.
4. How are the lives transforming of those closest to you by your church's emphasis on sanctification?
5. What are a few helpful ways your church could change to become a more effective sanctification community?
6. Are you satisfied with the sanctification practices of your church?

---

2 David Powlison "What is 'Ministry of the Word'"? Journal of Biblical Counseling, Winter 2003, Volume 21, Issue 2, 3–4.

9

Need More Than Preaching

The preaching event on Sunday morning and the working out of the preached Word during the week are not either/or activities. They both work together to help the Christian mature. The Christian life is not centered on the pulpit because the Christian lives his life chiefly everywhere else after the building door closes on Sunday. The person living by the preached Word on Sunday alone but not implementing contexts to work it into his or her soul will not mature the way God intends or the Bible teaches.

Community Living

There are 168 hours in our week. The preaching event is less than a one-hour soundbite out of each week. Even if we hear more than one sermon per week, it leaves us with over 165 hours to apply those sermons to our lives. Life outside the church building makes our communities the practical epicenter of our Christianity. Preaching has a prominent place in our lives, but it's only a supplemental prominence when talking about the change process. The New Testament does not make preaching the central focus of progressive sanctification.

The gospel has that role in our lives. To be more specific, Jesus Christ has a prominent and preeminent role in our lives, and preaching is one way to bring the gospel in view. The epicenter of our Christianity is a cross, a tomb, and a resurrected life. Preaching is an instrument to help us see, experience, and understand the gospel—the centrality of Christ. Preaching is a significant tool, but one of many. Moses seemed to understand the balance between sound preaching and sound application when he taught the children of Israel how to parent. He gave them the Word of God. Then he gave them practical instructions on how to take the Word of God to their homes so that they could apply it to their lives.

Public Preaching:

Hear, O Israel: The LORD our God, the LORD is one. You shall love the LORD your God with all your heart and with all your soul and with all your might. And these words that I command you today shall be on your heart.

Private Application:

You shall teach them diligently to your children, and shall talk of them when you sit in your house, and when you walk by the way, and when you lie down, and when you rise. You shall bind them as a sign on your hand, and they shall be as frontlets between your eyes. You shall write them on the doorposts of your house and your gates.

(Deuteronomy 6:4–9)

Preach and Application

Jesus' primary discipleship method took place in the context of people's lives where they were living. He did not disciple at the same place daily, and it was not primarily a monologue. Jesus took His discipleship outdoors and used those contexts to draw out His disciples. He discipled by using the physical world (e.g., birds, flowers, camels, nard) to illustrate the spiritual world (e.g., provision, sovereignty, anxiousness, worship, service, humility). Here is a classic illustration of how He went from the physical, concrete to the spiritual, specially addressing anxiety.

> Therefore I tell you, do not be anxious about your life, what you will eat or what you will drink, nor about your body, what you will put on. Is not life more than food, and the body more than clothing? Look at the birds of the air: they neither sow nor reap nor gather into barns, and yet your heavenly Father feeds them. Are you not of more value than they? And which of you by being anxious can add a single hour to his span of life? And why are you anxious about clothing? Consider the lilies of the field, how they grow: they neither toil nor spin, yet I tell you, even Solomon in all his glory was not arrayed like one of these. But if God so clothes the grass of the field, which today is alive and tomorrow is thrown into the oven, will he not much more clothe you, O you of little faith? Therefore do not be anxious, saying, "What shall we eat?" or "What shall we drink?" or "What shall we wear?" For the Gentiles seek after all these things, and your heavenly Father knows that you need them all. But seek first the kingdom of God and his righteousness, and all these things will be added to you. Therefore do not be anxious about tomorrow, for tomorrow will be anxious for itself. Sufficient for the day is its own trouble.
> (Matthew 6:25–34)

Jesus was so in tune with His world and audience that He never missed an opportunity to teach them God's practical and relevant ways. He did this through interpersonal interaction with His community. Sometimes, He would teach them through a stand-up monologue, and then later, He would practically work out His teaching lesson through interaction—two-way community dialogue.

Public Preaching:

Again he began to teach beside the sea. And a very large crowd gathered about him so that he got into a boat and sat in it on the sea, and the whole crowd was beside the sea on the land. And he was teaching them many things in parables, and in his teaching, he said to them: Listen! Behold, a sower went out to sow. And as he sowed, some seed fell along the path, and the birds came and devoured it. Other seed fell on rocky ground, where it did not have much soil, and immediately it sprang up since it had no depth of soil. And when the sun rose, it was scorched, and since it had no root, it withered away. Other seed fell among thorns, and the thorns grew up and choked it, and it yielded no grain. And other seeds fell into good soil and produced grain, growing up and increasing and yielding thirtyfold and sixtyfold and a hundredfold. And he said, He who has ears to hear, let him hear.

Private Application:

And when he was alone, those around him with the twelve asked him about the parables. And he said to them, To you has been given the secret of the kingdom of God, but for those outside everything is in parables, so that they may indeed see but not perceive, and may indeed hear but not understand, lest they should turn and be forgiven. And he said to them, Do you not understand this parable? How then will you understand all the parables?

(Mark 4:1-13)

Community Contexts

In verses 1-9, Jesus was teaching to a massive crowd from the pulpit, so to speak. In verses 10-13, He begins to unpack the teaching lesson in a personal, customized, relevant, and practical way for His community. The pulpit is a great place to exalt the Savior, expound the gospel, and call people to live in holiness. To be sure, God-ordained preaching for the proclamation of His Word is critical and prominent in our lives. It is the foolishness of preaching that confounds the wise and empowers the faithful (1 Corinthians 1:18).

In addition to great preaching, you also find in Scripture that it is in the living rooms of the community where the truths preached from the pulpit works out in the contexts of lives. You can encourage someone repeatedly from the pulpit to serve, and he may understand, personalize, and apply what you're saying. But if you bring a towel and basin to his living room and wash your friend's feet, you can be assured that he will never forget that one act of other-centered serving. (See John 13:15 and Matthew 26:13.) Helping others is where Jesus excelled. He contextualized His preached Word in the community of the believers. He did not let the preached Word stand alone. He modeled His message to drive home His points.

Practically Speaking

Mable has heard wonderful preaching over the past sixteen years of her life. Nearly every Sunday, she has been encouraged and enlightened, and she has been envisioned how to be a woman for God. Recently, a growing bitterness took root in her soul toward her church, her pastor, and some of her friends. The more she hears the beautiful truths from the Word declared from the pulpit, the more cynical and suspicious she becomes. She's seeing the discontinuity between the preached Word on Sunday and her marriage and family during the week. The dots are not practically connecting for her.

Sadly, her cynicism and suspicion are directed toward God—though she would never say it that way. She hoped for a different life and believed it would come by "going to church," as she put it. Her belief regarding the church is why she committed herself to God and the meetings of the church. She even took on a ministry in the church to help in whatever way she could. Her faith and practice were genuine. Mable loves God. But like a person asleep in a boat, only to awake hours later to find they drifted beyond the buoys, Mable's marriage has seemingly slipped past the point of no return. All the while, she is faithfully committed to her local church. Mable is not struggling with sound doctrine. She does not have a theological problem regarding her understanding of the Bible. What she has is a methodological problem.

Building a knowledge base through learning and growing in theological understanding is half the equation. Mable is getting good information on Sunday morning. It is consistently biblical, easy to understand, and well-delivered. Her problem and need is the other half of the solution. Her church has not provided or trained her to take the good Word preached and work it out in the milieu (contexts) of her life. She needs a way to ensure clear and practical application. The Lord did not design the Sunday church meeting to fulfill that part of what she must have. Mable is half-full: she knows the Word, but she does not have the equipping to apply it practically in ways that matter to her life, marriage, and other relationships. If she continues this way, she'll run on empty before long.

Call to Action

These questions will serve a person like Mable as she thinks through biblical solutions regarding comprehensive discipleship in the context of a local church community. As you reflect on this chapter, consider using these questions as a template for your thoughts. Ask these questions about your church. With all humility and charity, discuss them among your friends. I have designed them to bring clarity to your life and church community. They will challenge you to think through your motives for being part of your local church and your reasons for attending each week.

1. Is your church practically walking out a relational model of gospel-centered living versus a functional model that keeps you busy but doesn't build relationally? Is it relationally-centered or ministry-centered?
2. As you move from the pulpit to the periphery of the church, do all the lives of the church people model gospel-centered living? Are they being transformed in measurable and objective ways?
3. Is there an intentional plan implemented for disciple-making? Is it producing and reproducing disciple-makers?
4. Is there intentional, biblical care and accountability taking place in individual lives?
5. Are the men of the church leading their families? How do you know?
6. Is the faith of the church families exportable? (One of the ways to assess this is by talking to the church's teens. If the parents are being discipled well and responding to that discipleship, it will manifest in many—not all—of the parent's children.)
7. Do you experience biblical fellowship with a few

fellow members? (Biblical fellowship is sharing personally, intimately, and practically what God is doing in your life.)
8. Suppose you have a relational problem or situational difficulty. Are you comfortable and confident that you can go to your church leadership to describe your problem and receive competent care to walk you through it? Or do you seek solutions outside the local church because your local church cannot help you?
9. Why are you part of your local church? Are you transforming? Are your friends and family members experiencing transformation in proportion to their engagement with the local church?

10

A Perfect Dysfunctional Place

We have no choice but to be dysfunctional. We're all broken in different ways, as disorderedness is part of what it means to be born in Adam. Even on our best days, imperfections appear like a stain under white paint. Our collective fallenness is why the local church is so fabulous—a collection of broken people in a community of Christ-like disciple-makers seeking to draw closer to God and each other. The church is the place where you can be "just as I am." Though I'm not making a case for sinning your brains out or unleashing unbridled behavior, I'm a realist: we sin, and when we do, we're in a safe place to find the help we need. It's the perfect place to reveal our dysfunctional selves.

Time to Shine

Rather than trotting out our carefully edited representatives for public consumption, we can show people who we are while giving them hope in the masterpiece that God is producing. The local church is where all these future masterpieces gather, which is why our shared commonality with dysfunction does not discourage us. Only people without the gospel should have no hope. The born-again crowd lives in an ever-maturing, ordered reality with Christ as their head and His righteousness as our possession. We're not boasting as the world might boast, nor do we look down on others who have yet to taste the water that satisfies our souls. We mourn for them while doing all we can to reach them with the gospel. Meanwhile, we rejoice in the amazing grace that opened our eyes and changed our lives.

As you rejoice in the hope and help that only the gospel can bring, will you consider this list of words, some of the things we share in common? These are the negative things that come with our Adamic natures, the things we have yet to rid from our lives completely. However, because of the hope of Christ in us, this list also represents some of the things we should be discussing with our closest friends because there is wonder-working power in us, compelling us to be open and honest about the inhibitors that keep us from growing into a fuller man- or womanhood. Though these terms are negative, they do not overcome or overwhelm the psyche of those who believe.

Failure, disunity, hypocrisy, lust, fear, guilt, arrogance, dysfunction, gossip, disagreement, laziness, unforgiving, friction, jealousy, prejudice, anger, worry, arguments, shame, and competition.

Though the discussions with your church friends include more than these things, they must—at least—consist of these Adamic imperfections that have yet come under the obedience of Christ. What's in view here is not what we struggle with but that we must share our temptations, shortcomings, imperfections, hangups, and quirks with our closest network of friends. Perhaps you're asking, "Why should we be open with an appropriate number of friends with the determination and wisdom to entertain such things that will spur me on to love and good works?" If you are not sharing your innermost self with an appropriate friend, why not? What hinders you from making your local church a genuine sanctification hospital?

My Three Friends

BIFF, THE ANGRY GUY: Biff has been a small group member for over two years. From an outsider's perspective, he seems to have it together. Of course, that is his goal. He wants to maintain the perception of a stellar reputation. His small group does not know that he is an angry man. His wife and kids know it, and it has leaked out among a few friends. For the most part, his group does not know the real Biff. Biff is stuck on himself. He craves people's approval, so he controls his reputation tightly. He believes he must be on top of things and have it all together. Biff is an inch-deep, mile-wide Christian, but if there is not surgical intrusion from friends who are courageous, competent, and compassionate, Biff will continue with the deception, even if it causes generational dysfunction, as it most assuredly will.

BERT, THE ADDICTED GUY: Bert is a secret addict. He got hooked at seventeen. He's thirty-one now. He's been in a small group for a little over a year. He and Biff are friends, and they spend many weekends together because of their wives. Marge and Mable hit it off. Bert senses that Biff is not what he claims, but Bert thinks, "Shoot, who am I to judge? I've got this secret addiction." Bert plans to become clean for six months to a year before he tells Marge. He thinks that if he can kick the habit, he can talk about his addiction as though it was something in his past rather than a current struggle. He wants to maintain his reputation, project humility before the group by confessing (a past conflict), and gain some accountability in case his temptation comes knocking again. His plan is similar to Biff's. In a word, he wants to control the situation. Rather than partnering with the foolishness and weakness of the gospel, Biff and Bert plan to correct their problems through self-reliant means (1 Corinthians 1:18–25).

BRICE, THE HUMBLE GUY: Then Brice enters the group. He is a young Christian who has not learned the—deceptive—ropes yet: Biff and Bert have not contaminated him yet. Hypocrisy and the art of deception are not for the novice. Brice is still wet behind the ears. He believes in the Bible and talks as though it is the best thing since sliced bread. He's a newbie to small group life. Biff and Bert have measured transparency. They drip out certain things about themselves during small group to show humility. They give the perception they are in the group, but they are not. Brice is amazed at their honesty and openness. From his perspective, it radically differs from the nonsense in his office, e.g., gossip around the water cooler, power ties, power lunches, and the survival of the fittest race to the top mindset. The saying goes, "It's easy to impress the fifth graders." Brice, the small group fifth-grader, is impressed and grateful for his new group.

Suppressed Transparency

> Behold, you have sinned against the LORD, and be sure your sin will find you out.
>
> (Numbers 32:23)

You can imagine what a surprise it was to Brice the night Biff's wife, Mable, blurted out, "I can't take it anymore. I'm leaving Biff. He's intolerable." From that point, she shared his many unexposed secrets through tears. She talked about the threats, his condemning ways, and even the physical abuse of her and the children. It was not a pretty picture. Sadly, it did not have to come out the way it did. All of us struggle with suppressed transparency. Like Adam before

LOCAL CHURCH

us, our native tendency is to grab fig leaves and cover up the shame in our lives (Genesis 3:7). Hiding sin is a mild form of insanity. Go back and reread the above list of negative Adamic traits. It is our list; it represents only part of who we are. Why do we want to pretend those things do not belong to us? Why do we want to suppress our transparency?

> Do not be deceived: "Bad company ruins good morals."
>
> (1 Corinthians 15:33)

DISCIPLING
Teaching What You Learn

HOMEWORK
Customized to the Unique Person

PRAYER
BIBLE STUDY
Speaking and Listening to God

MICRO SESSIONS
Life Over Coffee Content

SERVING OTHERS
Practically Caring for Others

SUPPORTING COMMUNITY
LOC Likeminded Friends

Good Companions
1 Corinthians 15:33

CHURCH MEETINGS
Actively Engaging Your Church

BRING A FRIEND
Invite a Friend to Counseling

SMALL GROUP LIFE
Koinonia in Church Groups

Truthfully, there are more things to add to the list, as mind-boggling as that may appear. Depravity does not have boundaries, and complete insulation from sin's encroachments is impossible. People have implemented harsh aesthetic and isolating practices into their lives, only to realize that you cannot separate from the world because the world is in our hearts. Christians' collective fallenness is why a reliable company of friends is essential. Biff and Bert are not good companions, and they may corrupt Brice if things do not change. Think about how insane it is to participate in a small group that talks about sanctification but refuses to let the group in on their dirty little secrets. All Christian groups are the same; it's a struggle to open up about the more in-depth struggles of our lives. But what are our options? If you participate in a small group, here are three common hindrances to keep you from a productive small group life experience.

Everyone Is Afraid

Rarely will someone be like Brice; most people yield to the temptation to hide their shame. When Lucia and I began the complicated process of looking for a church, we did not put finding a transparent, intentional, sanctified, small group on our list of non-negotiables. The reason is simple: we have never belonged to a local church that aggressively pursued each other this way. We have been in groups discussing this kind of vibrant life together, but there is a difference between talking about intentional sanctification and practically practicing it. If you want what I am describing, stop complaining about it—if you are—and develop it by your self-disclosing example, with all wisdom and discretion. When we landed in our new local church, we were not disappointed. The small group life was not that great, so we prayed for some like-minded people to cross our paths—individuals who embrace a transparent pursuit of mutual sanctification for the glory of God.

Devaluing the Community

Don't settle for anything less than a group of friends who want to do intentional sanctification together. Did you know you can be dissatisfied with superficiality and still be humble? You don't have to be mad about it, but you can be righteously dissatisfied. If you're afraid of opening up, ask God to give you the favor to where your desire for this kind of community trumps your fear of being exposed. Biff and Bert's relationships with God and family are deteriorating daily. They live in unexposed sin while participating in a small group designed to fight against what they are hiding. It's like becoming sicker in the hospital; it is not supposed to be that way. Biff and Bert do not understand or want to understand the value of community life. Fortunately, Biff's wife had enough grit to spill the beans. Though it would have been better for Biff to humble himself, his wife mercifully was willing to do what he was afraid to do for himself. Any loving spouse would call the doctor if her spouse were sick. If you try to grow your sanctification outside of the body of Christ, you need to adjust your view of the body of Christ. Growth outside the body is not possible.

Succumbing to Temptation

> No temptation has overtaken you that is not common to man. God is faithful, and he will not let you be tempted beyond your ability, but with the temptation he will also provide the way of escape, that you may be able to endure it.
> (1 Corinthians 10:13)

Some of you reading this have hidden sins in your lives. It's hidden from your spouse, and it's hidden from your friends. You do not want to be exposed, and we all know why because we're just like you. Would you please pray right now? Ask God to give you an enabling favor to talk to your small group leader or close friend immediately so that you can confess what is going on in your life. All your struggles are not unique to you. We all struggle in similar ways. The good news is that nothing you struggle with is outside God's transforming grace. If your temptation is to suppress transparency, will you change that pattern in your life today? Trust God. Die to self. Be honest for His glory, your well-being, and the effectiveness of your church.

Call to Action

1. Describe the relationships in your local church. Are they aggressive about being intentionally intrusive in each others' lives?
2. If they are a vibrant community, how did that happen? If the church is not, why do you believe they are not?
3. What is your role in helping your church mature in its sanctification? What will you do to be part of the solution in your church?
4. What one point stood out to you in this chapter? What specific and practical thing will you do in response?
5. Will you share this chapter with a friend and discuss how you can make a difference in your church?

11

A Crazy Idea

One-to-one interaction is the most efficient way to help another person change. For too many believers, discipleship in a community, in the context of a local church, is not the place where you see this kind of intentional reciprocality. Favorite books and popular preachers become our disciplers, which is not God's best, no matter how wonderful the celebrity preacher or your favorite book is because those means of grace are passive instead of surgically illuminating and uniquely transformative. Nothing displaces a competent, caring friend who can exegete you with God's Word in a customizable way while bringing solutions that fit who you are and what's happening in your life.

A Crisis of Hurting

Some Christians sometimes isolate themselves while cuddling with books and famous online people, hoping to find safe, private, personal, marriage, or family transformation. Though the temptation is understandable, it's not primarily the Bible's way for one another sanctification. The most frequent email requests I receive from people are questions regarding specific situations in their lives. Each morning that I wake up, there are emails from real people with real problems, looking for practical answers. They are not interested in what a book says.

These hurting people don't want to hear another sermon. They're looking for someone who will take the time to listen to them, understand them, and give them valuable biblical feedback. Even the best Christian books and well-crafted sermons cannot do what a Christian can do when sitting in front of a person, offering real answers. This kind of vision for discipleship requires work. It needs the discipler to dedicate real time to an individual. It requires patience, courage, discernment, and wisdom. It requires the struggling person to be humble, open, honest, and vulnerable.

Discipling with Dialogue

One-to-one interaction is how Jesus built His team and followers. When you read the four gospels, you notice how Jesus rarely taught in a monologue-type format (teaching). Though He was a teacher, the Bible does not give us a lot of scenes showing Him teaching. If you pull out the Sermon on the Mount, you will not find much monologue teaching from Him (Matthew 5-7). Using monologue was not His specialty. Jesus was a dialogue guy.

He spent nearly all His time interacting with folks, showing them how to be Christlike. One of the most significant weaknesses of the modern-day church is how we've given discipleship to famous authors, Bible studies, podcasts, and sermons. While there is a place for media for discipling others, it should not be the primary method. The monologue discipleship model has created two adverse side effects on the church.

Side Effect #1 has led to the biblical counseling (BC) movement, especially para-church organizations like mine. The BC movement deals with real people with real problems in a practical way—similar to the way Jesus did. The church seems to be more focused on teaching. Still, when somebody has a problem, they refer the hurting person to a—so-called—professional because they don't have the time, resources, or expertise to deal with sanctification issues. Read that sentence again. Did it sound odd to you? The church seems preoccupied with programs and ministry demands while—perhaps—assuming their people know how to counsel themselves.

Side Effect #2 is a breakdown in the community because of an isolationist mindset where people feed themselves in private. People retreat to their books, podcasts, and personal devotions to find answers to their most perplexing problems. Rather than running to the community, the temptation is to become remote, insecure, and guarded about their authentic selves. There is a distrust of the community. Confidentiality is one of the more frequent questions individuals ask me: "I don't want anyone to know what I'm going through." Essentially, they say, "I want you to fix me so I can go back to church." It is as though everyone wants a private room to separate from each other until they are doing better.

Up in Your Business

You see a different picture when you read how Christ built His church or how the early churches poured themselves into each other. Read Acts 2:42-47 about the early church. See if you can "feel the community" in that passage. The people have all things in common. There is mutual sharing, caring, and communal intrusion into each other's lives.

> And they devoted themselves to the apostles' teaching and fellowship, to the breaking of bread and the prayers. And awe came upon every soul and many wonders and signs were being done through the apostles. And all who believed were together and had all things in common. And they were selling their possessions and belongings and

distributing the proceeds to all, as any had a need. And day by day, attending the temple together and breaking bread in their homes, they received their food with glad and generous hearts, praising God and having favor with all the people. And the Lord added to their number day by day those who were being saved.

(Acts 2:42-47)

The early church does not have a lecturer-to-student feel. It does not have the hurting-isolationists-with-a-book feel. A sense of transparency, vulnerability, and humility bleeds through the passage. Gospel-centered people have nothing to protect and nothing to hide. They have one common goal, laid out in three parts. The goal is Jesus, and the parts are as follows:

- **PERSONAL:** I want to know more about Jesus.
- **COMMUNAL:** I want to experience Jesus's life with each other mutually.
- **EVANGELISTIC:** I hope to share Jesus with people who do not know Him.

What Did Jesus Do?

The early Christians were in each other's business, and what they were doing had a far different feel than the guardedness of the average Christian today. Regarding matters of the heart, today's Christians prefer getting fixed in private, only to resurface later to do community with fellow believers. The New Testament Christian was not that insecure or image-conscious. They came just as they were, integrated with fellow strugglers, and mutually matured in a community. They were well aware of what was going on in the lives of those around them—including their thought lives.

The New Testament believers learned this gospelized living from Jesus' leaders. The folks Jesus trained passed on what they learned to others (2 Timothy 2:2). How did the Savior do it? His primary discipleship style was living with the folks He trained. Jesus knew the buckshot, monologue approach would not get the job done. He needed to get with the people, love them, learn about them, and lead them from within their social context—discipling within the milieu.

Unique Unpacking

You will not get to know a person the way you should by attending a safe and sterile Bible study or a church meeting staring at the back of a person's head. I am not saying biblical training and studies are unnecessary or ineffective. Knowing the Bible is essential, but growing in Bible knowledge and being Christlike are different. Paul was one of the most learned students of his day. He was a Bible scholar. But poor Paul did not know how to take what he knew about the Bible and live it biblically (Acts 22:3). Somebody had to teach him.

Nicodemus was another learned Bible student who stumbled all over the new birth. He knew a lot but was unaware of how to take the Old Testament, which he had, and practicalize it into his life. He, like Paul, needed someone to teach him (John 3:1-8). The Samaritan woman was also well-trained by her culture and religion. She was a hybrid in more ways than one. Her religious training was just as deficient as Paul's and Nick's. She needed someone to cuddle up beside her to unpack her. Jesus did not send her to a Bible study or ask her to listen to a sermon.

Christ exegeted her on the spot—at a well. He took a real person and got into her real business by customizing the gospel for her while hanging in her social environment (John 4:7-26). Paul, Nick, and the Samaritan woman had

A Crazy Idea

one thing in common. They met Jesus in the milieu—in the natural social environment in which they lived. Jesus interacted with all of His counselees where they lived. His discipleship method positioned Him to be an effective discipler. He did not offer Paul, Nick, or the Samaritan woman an excellent book to read. He read them and told them what He was learning. He pulled this off because He spent time with them. He knew them.

Take It to the Streets

Too many leaders meet their people at the church building or in other environments that are ministerially sterile or artificial. They listen to their problems, offer counsel, make a book recommendation, and send them on their way. It does not work well. I'm in a similar boat. When people call me, they want to bring their world into my office to converse. I'm glad they are willing to come; I'm happy to serve them in the minimal way I can help someone.

TIME & RELATIONSHIP PRIORITIES

1 - The Father & Jesus

2 - Peter, James, John

3 - The Nine Disciples

4 - Mary, Martha, et.al.

5 - The Multitudes

6 - The Unregenerate

Jesus would give anyone His care, but only a few people His undivided attention.

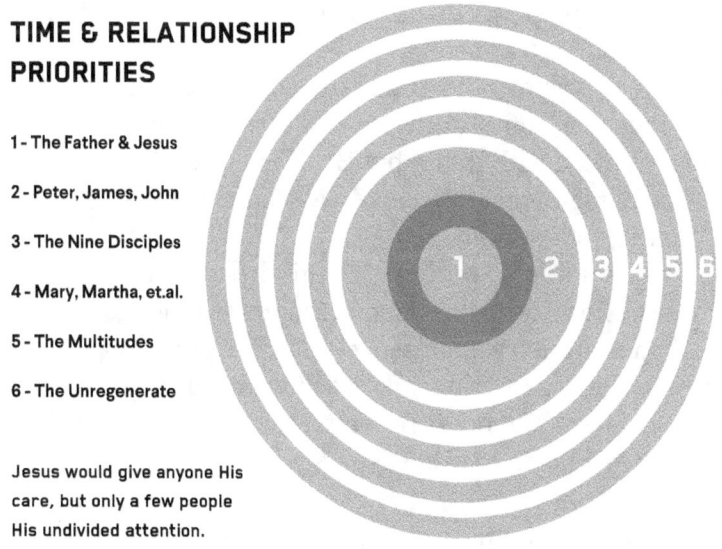

But this puts me in a dilemma because I cannot help them comprehensively. They need someone onsite in their lives to serve them, observe them, and bring discipleship care to them. Jesus spent time eating, drinking, and relaxing with His friends. He did life with those whom He developed. Jesus knew them inside and out. He was aware of the nuances of their lives. What He got out of them by living with them was priceless information.

Living Like Jesus

The local church is the closest approximation in our culture today to what the Savior had in His day. Jesus lived in a small group, and within that small group, He divided His leadership development time differently. His calendar looked like the following:

1. Jesus: He spent time with the Father, receiving refreshment, challenges, and envisioning.
2. Peter, James, and John: These guys got the top spots on His calendar.
3. Other apostles: He then spent time developing the rest of His team.
4. Mary, Martha, and other friends: He never forgot about the community. He had many friends and was often with them, but He did not neglect building the main guys who would carry the mission and vision.
5. Multitudes: He preached to this group and occasionally broke some bread to feed them and other ministry efforts. (Delegation Tip: His team did the distributing, and He did the multiplying.)
6. Pharisees and other resisters: Occasionally, He did apologetic and evangelistic work.

Jesus was a methodical man on a mission. His mission had

two primary parts: die for the sins of the world and get His main guys envisioned and equipped to carry the gospel message to the church. We only have to do one part of His mission as outlined in Ephesians 4:12–14. However, in our zeal to get the gospel message out, we can be ineffective in developing our infrastructure—the local church. We provide books and Bible studies while assuming our people are practicalizing the Bible into their lives. We don't follow up well. A decade later, you learn a leader's marriage is on the brink of divorce, and you're perplexed. How did that happen?

- They attended our church for two decades.
- They taught Sunday school forever.
- They led mission outreach every year.
- They are respected and loved by our church family.
- They counseled dozens of our people.

We say, "I never saw it coming." We were not involved in their lives. It's a miscalculation of the doctrines of sin and sanctification, and it's an assumption that sound preaching, good books, and ministry busyness were what they needed. Jesus did not leave sanctification solely to the preaching of the Word. The best discipleship is hands-on discipleship. We are two thousand years removed from when the Savior trained His group, and His method is still the best. Yes, we have better technology. We have excelled in theological precision regarding our beliefs through councils and creeds. We have written a dizzying amount of books and Bible study materials.

Build Relationally

Even with all of these things, none of them can supplant building relationally, one-to-one, the way Jesus did, with another human being. The functional centrality of the gospel working practically in the lives of the local church is today's most significant need. The way I seek to serve my church with this vision is pretty simple. There are three groups of people in my life today: our family, our church, and everyone else. I know bits and pieces, more and less, and this and that about group three. I don't know them well and have minimal impact on their lives. Then there is my family and church. I cannot even begin to tell you what I know about them, what they know about me, and how we engage each other. Here are some examples:

- We have sinned against each other.
- We have been angry with each other.
- We have prayed for each other.
- We have cried with each other.
- We have laughed with each other.
- We have secretly judged each other.
- We have confronted each other.
- We have encouraged each other.
- We have said hurtful things to each other.
- We have spent hundreds of hours in different contexts with each other.

The local church is a dangerous and vulnerable group of people for the glory of God. After all this interaction, we are still not as effective as we need to be. I'm not discouraged. No, not at all. It's sanctification progress. It took the Savior three years, with fewer distractions, to get His group up to speed.

Call to Action

1. How should you change your family to make it a more effective sanctification community?
2. How must you change to help your church become a more effective sanctification community?
3. Pick a person that you can have this type of life with and invite them into your life, marriage, or family. Will you contact that person today?

12

Do You Fight Fires?

The best discipleship soul care happens in a community, not isolated, artificial settings where there is a disconnection between the person and the community. God can change lives in one-and-done or a season of meetings, and no reasonable person would argue against the good Lord doing just that, but the most compelling soul care needs time, people, and context. Body-to-body ministry is the primary way change happens, placing a requirement on every believer to do all they can to equip themselves to make our local churches more effective discipleship communities.

Doing Denny's

A few years ago, a man called, asking if I would mentor him. He asked if I would meet with him once or twice a month for discipleship purposes. I understood his question but was struggling with how to tell him that what he was asking would not deliver what he wanted. The only discipleship model he knew was the one-to-one, in-a-silo model that has become prevalent in the church over the past few decades. It is an insufficient model, though it adapts well to our fast-paced lifestyles and busy calendars. Adaptability is its most significant feature. If you are busy and do not have the time to dig into the muck of a person's life in the context of community, the every-so-often, one-to-one routine is a quick and safe option for you.

Ineffectiveness is its greatest weakness. I call this "doing Denny's," named after the restaurant chain, not because of any affiliation or affection for the restaurant chain, but because it rolls off the tongue. The question is not whether meeting with someone in any context is helpful because it can be. The real issue is whether meeting with someone outside of that person's regular life settings is the best option to help him transform into Christlikeness. These abbreviated and artificial meetings have a limited effect but not a full effect, which is the difference. The early church's discipleship model was relational, holistic, communal, and in the milieu.

> And all who believed were together and had all things in common. And they were selling their possessions and belongings and distributing the proceeds to all, as any had need. And day by day, attending the temple together and breaking bread in their homes.
>
> (Acts 2:44–46)

Totally Messed Up

We must consider several things regarding best practices for change, such as the doctrine of total depravity. People who only practice one-to-one soul care outside of real-life contexts need to reflect more on the overall effects of sin in their lives. The Bible teaches the total depravity of the human race. Total depravity means radical corruption. We do note the difference between total depravity and utter depravity. To be utterly depraved is to be as wicked as one could be. Hitler was extremely degenerate, but he could have been worse than he was. I am a sinner, but I could sin more often and more severely than I do. I am not utterly depraved, but I am totally depraved.

> *For total depravity means that I and everyone else are depraved or corrupt in the totality of our being. There is no part of us that is left untouched by sin. Our minds, our wills, and our bodies are affected by evil. We speak sinful words, do sinful deeds, have impure thoughts. Our very bodies suffer from the ravages of sin.*
>
> —R. C. Sproul

Carefully think through what Sproul is saying. We are not only worse off than we ever imagined but are capable of doing things that are more wicked than anything we have done up to this moment (Romans 3:10–12). If the only context in which you are meeting with a person is one-to-one, in an environment outside their everyday community, you will limit your ability to know and impact them. This lack of complete relational care will tempt you to frustration when they do not change.

A lack of long-term, effectual change is one of the biggest reasons I do not prefer counseling as a stand-alone event disconnected from a community of believers who can provide ongoing, reciprocal care. The overwhelming majority of the people who change do so because they were involved in more than a counseling event or a counseling season. The doctrine of human depravity demands more than a counseling event or season for actual life change.

I'm F.I.N.E.

When you meet a person and ask how they are doing, they say they are doing fine, good, or okay. As one of my friends says, "The word 'fine' means "feelings inside never expressed." He is right. We will always and forever put our best foot forward when asked how we are doing. There are several reasons for this, some of which are good, though there is a deeper problem. We may say we are "fine" because it is quick and easy, but we are never actually fine, and to compound this problem, we are never fully aware of how "un-fine" we are. None of us have enough self-awareness to inform ourselves how to be self-suspicious. Remember total depravity? The word total means total. We are totally depraved. Our thinking is not entirely in line with the gospel, and it never will be until we meet Jesus when we receive our body upgrade.

- "All the ways of a man are pure in his own eyes, but the Lord weighs the spirit" (Proverbs 16:2).
- "There are those who are clean in their own eyes but are not washed of their filth" (Proverbs 30:12).
- "There is a way that seems right to a man, but its end is the way to death" (Proverbs 14:12).

Even on our best days, when we are operating at optimal levels, we do not know ourselves the way we need to be understood. We have Adamic blinders that guarantee blind spots. Personal blindness makes discipling someone outside of their day-to-day community an insufficient way of doing sanctification because they will never be able to give you all the information you need to help them (Romans 8:26). If I am counseling a spouse and the other spouse is not present, I automatically know there is another story that I will never be able to perceive until I talk with the person not present.

> The one who states his case first seems right, until the other comes and examines him.
> (Proverbs 18:17)

For me, it is the worst possible counseling scenario. These deficiencies in soul care are what I wanted to communicate to my friend. I tried to care for him, but I wanted him to be in a sanctification community where people knew him daily. Caring for him at "Denny's" on an every-other-week basis is better than nothing. But it is not as good as seeing him at his local church, in his home, with his wife and family, and in the many other contexts that real community offers.

Firefighter or Life Changer?

I planted, Apollos watered, but God gave the growth.
(1 Corinthians 3:6)

Christians are acutely aware that if a person changes, God's grace enables and empowers the transformation. We are planters and waterers; only the Lord can bring change. The question for us is not about who does the changing but how we cooperate with the Changer of Lives in His transformation process. Thus, each discipler must decide on the kind of soul care they want to provide. There is no one way or one correct answer for discipleship. There are many options. Jesus used several. He determined the care needed by the person He was interacting with and the type of need in their lives.

- He did not provide soul care for some people, as we see in John 2:24–25.
- He did provide soul care if those who needed it and would turn from their wicked ways as seen in Matthew 23:37.
- He offered advice but did not extend Himself beyond that in Luke 18:18–23.
- He did not provide care to His family if they were not going to do the Lord's will as seen in Matthew 12:48–50.
- He reached out to the community through others but did not personally interact with them as seen in Matthew 14:13–21.

- He provided instruction to the community but found it wiser to get away from them as seen in Matthew 14:22-23.
- He spent most of His time with individuals whom He could replicate into leaders as seen in Matthew 4:18-19.

Jesus implemented a "whosoever-will" method for discipleship, meaning He did not withhold care from anyone, but everybody did not receive the same kind of attention from Him. Providing the same in-depth equipping to every person who knocks on your door is impossible. Different levels of soul care are one of the many things I appreciate about Jesus. He was discerning and courageous enough to know who would get His best discipleship time. He was unafraid to say hard things to people, even if it made them mad (John 11:21) or if they left Him without life change (Mark 10:17-27).

Everybody can receive your care, but not everyone can receive your ongoing attention. If you cannot discern the difference and divide people accordingly, the requests for help will overrun you, and areas of your personal life will unravel. Because my friend did not attend my church, it was unwise for me to set up ongoing and unending meetings in artificial contexts when he could receive better soul care from those who did life with him at his local church. I could give him some tips. I could point him in the right direction. I could encourage him about getting long-term discipleship care in the community context, but I could not provide adequate, comprehensive care because we did not do life together.

Sanctification Contexts

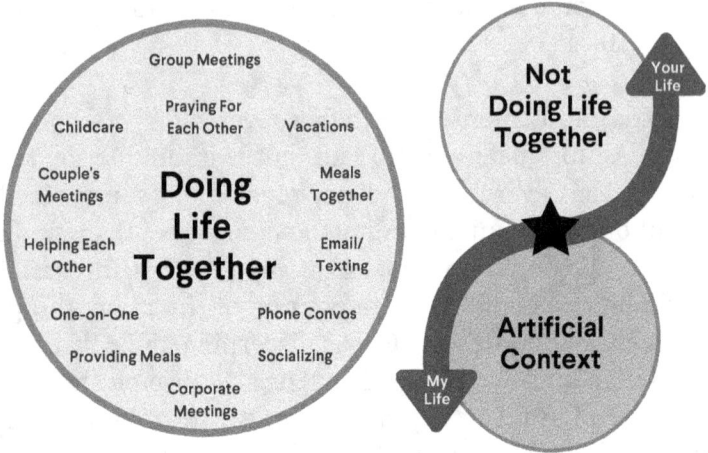

The infographic gives you a glance at the two discipleship models I'm describing. These are the two most common ways soul care happens in the church today. The two circles on the right are meetings prearranged between two people who do not do life together on a daily/weekly basis. These kinds of meetings are more artificial than real. Let's call them Mable and Marge, both married with children. They meet every two weeks at a local coffee shop for about ninety minutes. Mable is discipling Marge, who is in a difficult marriage, and her teenage children are apathetic toward the church. Her husband has anger issues, and Marge bounces from fear to bitterness to anger, depending on the week.

All Mable can do is fight fires. She has no leverage over the whole family and no insight into the fundamental dynamics of the home. She does not see how Marge blows up when at her wit's end or how her husband checks out because of her double-minded behavior (James 1:5-6). Marge will talk about getting frustrated, but that is a far cry from reality. Seeing is believing, but Mable cannot see. She can only take Marge's perspective because they are "doing Denny's." At best, Mable can give advice and send Marge on her way, hoping a nugget of truth dropped will slow down the dysfunctional spin of the home.

The problem with this model is that their primary interaction is in a context that does not resemble how they live. Artificial settings describe counseling sessions. Counseling is another "doing Denny's" model of discipleship. The artificial context model leaves you guessing, speculating, drawing conclusions, assuming, and hoping you understand because you are never the proverbial fly on the wall of their lives. The second model—on the left—gives you "wall space" to hang out with those you are discipling. You are not doing Denny's. You are doing life together with another person, couple, family, or small group.

Doing Life

This second, more extensive circle is how I historically have led small groups. In the doing life together model, you see thirteen different contexts in which you can connect with someone. You will not do all of those things with every member of your small group, but you could potentially do any of those things, and if you are doing small group life well, you will be doing most of them, and those you're developing will be modeling your leadership. You cannot do this kind of life with every person you meet. Not even Jesus could sustain this level of discipleship with everyone. He had a small group of twelve people. They received His most comprehensive care. Nobody was left behind if they did not want to be left behind, but everybody did not get prime time with Him.

Discipleship is a two-way street. It is not a uni-directional model. Reciprocal soul care is the primary reason for doing life together: we need someone caring for our souls too. I do not want to meet at Denny's with someone to care for me if they are not caring for my wife and children simultaneously. There is no way for them to know me if they do not know my wife and children. If you want to know me, spend time with them and me.

My family will give you a more accurate description of the kind of person I am than meeting with me alone. Not only will they help you to help me, but you will find out quickly what kind of husband and father I am. They are "Exhibit A" to the leadership and care I provide in our home. Please don't ask the farmer at Denny's to describe his garden to you, the fruit of his hands. Walk into his fields and examine them yourself. It will not take you long to get an accurate bead on the kind of person you are discipling.

Call to Action

1. Are you a firefighter or a soul care provider? What are the differences?
2. Why is meeting with someone sporadically and in artificial contexts not the best discipleship model?
3. What are the advantages of meeting someone in multiple settings?

13

Are You Committed?

The local church is the dearest place on earth, outside of our unique families. It is the one place where the body of Christ can gather to celebrate their King while caring for each other in all the various contexts possible. It is an amazing means of grace, where families can gather to spur one another to love and good works. Though all Christians should commit themselves to a local gathering, it's not the case. What about you? Are you committed to your local church? Do you make it easy for your fellow church members to care for you?

The Dearest Place

Biff and Mable have been struggling in their marriage for years. Biff took his first sip of alcohol when he was nineteen years old. Biff never stopped drinking. He's forty-one years old today and a closet alcoholic. Mable pled with Biff for over a decade to stop his drinking. He's a mean drunk. She stopped begging eleven years ago. They came to counseling after Biff lost his third job in the past year, and though he did not know it, Mable had been living in adultery for the previous four years. A lack of connectivity to the local church became apparent at the core of their problems—

though there were many of them. They were doing life outside a caring community of Christlike disciple-makers at every turn.

Sadly, Biff and Mable did not see the importance of connecting to their local church. Their obliviousness was enough for me to pause and reflect. Do you love your local church? Are you practically connected to your church? Who is the person in your church that knows what's going on with your life? Charles Spurgeon preached a message about the local church called "the dearest place on earth." Spurgeon saw the church as the center of the Christian's life. Our individualistic, isolated culture that prefers to connect in cyberspace is a universe away from the culture in Spurgeon's day. Today, the individual—in his cyber silo—is at the center of it all while the church sits on the periphery. A typical local church is a weak competitor in the fight for calendar space in the Christian's life—a far cry from the early church.

> And they devoted themselves to the apostles' teaching and fellowship, to the breaking of bread and the prayers. And awe came upon every soul, and many wonders and signs were being done through the apostles. And all who believed were together and had all things in common. And they were selling their possessions and belongings and distributing the proceeds to all, as any had need. And day by day, attending the temple together and breaking bread in their homes, they received their food with glad and generous hearts, praising God and having favor with all the people. And the Lord added to their number day by day those who were being saved.
>
> (Acts 2:42–47)

Imagine if Biff and Mable had the values of the early church. I'll list three of them for us while challenging ourselves to examine our life to see how we compare to the first followers of Christ.

- **Community**—*all things common:* The community life of the believer lives out in reciprocal relationships. We cannot experience the full measure of our church if we are not seeking to live with one another in a community. Genuine, authentic, transparent, and honest relationships are essential to life in a community. What parts of your life do you hold back from those who should know you best? Is your church life experience more about a rote duty that fills a spot or gospel joy that spills out on others?
- **Service**—*distributing proceeds to all:* Giving our lives away without demanding anything in return is at the heart of the gospel. We are stewards of God's stuff rather than an owner of our stuff. And our stuff also includes us. We are not our own (1 Corinthians 6:19-20). Are you joyfully giving yourself away to your local church? What does sacrificial giving look like in your life?
- **Worship**—*praising God:* God wired us for worship. Worshipers are who we are and what we do. The vertical relationship between us and God is the greatest commandment of all (Matthew 22:36-40). Our adoration and affection for God determine how we live out our lives in the context of our local churches. Is your Sunday church meeting experience primarily a celebration of the Father, Son, and Spirit or another purpose? How are you characterized: a person of praise or lacking passion for God?

A Body Thing

One of the sadder by-products of the seeker-sensitive movement is the creation of a new category for Christians, the church attendee. We have never had such an accommodating category for the Christian in the church's history. This lack of commitment to the local church is, in part, what keeps me in business as a para-church organization. It is rare for me to counsel people actively involved in their local church and living in authentic, reciprocal relationships with other genuine believers. Active church engagement is the point Biff and Mable missed. Unless I'm going to become someone's life coach, I cannot provide long-term care in the way they need care. No para-church organization can do this; God does not call a para-church organization to do this. Long-term soul care is the job of the local church.

Please permit me to make it personal: I will not stop sinning in this life. I wish I could stop sinning, but I'm a realist. I'm a Christian who sins, and because of my sinfulness, I need external care from others. My sinfulness is one of the primary reasons I am committed to my local church. Biff, Mable, and Rick need help. For the glory of God and the sake of my wife and our children, I plead with my local church—specific close friends in the church—to come alongside me to care for me so I can mature into the man God wants me to be. I cannot fathom being a regular attendee.

> And they were not devoted to the pastors' teaching or fellowship or the breaking of bread and the prayers. Grumbling came upon every soul, and many cynically critiqued the things done through the leadership. They were individuals, having little in common. And they were selling all kinds of stuff to keep the proceeds because they were greedy.

> *Whenever they felt like it, they attended the church meetings, beating it to the restaurants afterward. They received their food with glad and gluttonous hearts, superficially praising God because they craved the favor of all the people. And the Lord added more attendees to their number daily, and the church continued to weaken.*
>
> (Acts 2:42–47, revisited)

A Pastor's Appeal

> *Obey your leaders and submit to them, for they are keeping watch over your souls, as those who will have to give an account. Let them do this with joy and not with groaning, for that would be of no advantage to you.*
>
> (Hebrews 13:17)

A pastor is a man called to care for his people. The Bible elevates the seriousness of the pastor's call by stating that God will hold him accountable for how he cares for his members. Peter weighed in on the seriousness of the call by using the metaphor of a shepherd and his sheep.

> *Shepherd the flock of God that is among you, exercising oversight, not under compulsion, but willingly, as God would have you; not for shameful gain, but eagerly; not domineering over those in your charge, but being examples to the flock.*
>
> (1 Peter 5:2–3)

James came from another angle while speaking on the seriousness of the call when he said God would hold teachers to a higher standard of accountability.

> Not many of you should become teachers, my brothers, for you know that we who teach will be judged with greater strictness.
>
> (James 3:1)

Once upon a time, I was part of a pastoral team in a local church. These verses, along with a few others, helped me to understand the seriousness of God's call on my life. Caring for people is essential to God and is important to me. However, it is not humanly possible to care for everyone. A person who attempts to care for everyone will be unable to care for anyone well. But when people are committed to our local church, we were humbled by their commitment and sought to bring consistent and practical care to them. However, there was another group of people where the lines were not as clear. They were the uncommitted ones. It is hard to discern what level of care I should provide for them. At times, I prayed this way:

> Dear Father, I love these people, but no matter how much I teach or appeal, they won't commit to our body. Lord, would you be so kind to change their hearts? Would you persuade them to plug into our local church or lead them to another one where they would be in faith to commit? Please don't hold me accountable for them if they are unwilling to commit to our care. Will you give me the words to say to them that would encourage them to engage us or find another church? Amen!

The Uncommitted

There were questions that rolled around my mind when a person attended but never committed to our church. Though I did not ask the questions the way they are listed below, they do convey the ideas I tried to communicate to the occasional attendee who would never commit.

- Do you believe in what we are doing as a church? Do you understand and believe in the vision and values of our church? If so, are you willing to commit?
- We are not the only church in town. It is okay if you do not attend here. There are other churches you can find. Please be free to look elsewhere. Though we would love to have you, you can go somewhere else.
- What would you like to do? I need to know what you are in faith to do. Are you in faith to be here, to engage with us? Or do you believe you should look for another church?
- Where you land is not the point, but settling somewhere is essential. How can I help you get plugged into this church or another? Please let me know how I can serve you.
- God holds me responsible for how I care for our people. It is impossible to commit to every person who walks through our doors. However, we are eager and excited to invest in those who believe they are supposed to be here. Do you believe you should be here?

As a pastor, I desired to commit to those who were part of our local church. However, their commitment was the key to the how, when, why, and what of my pastoral care. God was holding me accountable to some people, but He was not holding me responsible to everyone. Appealing for commitment was why we tried to draw a line so we could work hard, wisely, efficiently, and with much joy without sacrificing our families. I am not saying we had cornered the market on how to do church. We were constantly changing, but at the end of the day, it had to look like something, and we had clear ideas of how to care for people, so we presented our way and asked for a commitment. Sometimes, people did not prefer our care model, which was okay. We praised God for how other biblical churches provided care, and if an attendee did not want to commit to us, we would help them find them a place where they could fully invest their lives.

Not about Us

Ultimately, the church is not yours or mine; it's God's. Likewise, a local church does not grow because of what we can scheme and manage. There is no magical formula for achieving a vibrant church life. God gave us gifts we must apply in the wisest ways we know while trusting Him for the results. Biff and Mable were regular attendees at their local church. Their commitment to their local church was similar to their commitment to their marriage: it was weak. They never fully engaged in the dearest place on earth for the glory of God, the benefit of themselves, and the blessing of others.

> His divine power has granted to us all things that pertain to life and godliness, through the knowledge of him who called us to his own glory and excellence, by which he has granted to us his precious and very great promises, so that through them you may become partakers of the divine nature, having escaped from the corruption that is in the world because of sinful desire.
>
> For this very reason, make every effort to supplement your faith with virtue, and virtue with knowledge, and knowledge with self-control, and self-control with steadfastness, and steadfastness with godliness, and godliness with brotherly affection, and brotherly affection with love. For if these qualities are yours and are increasing, they keep you from being ineffective or unfruitful in the knowledge of our Lord Jesus Christ.
>
> (2 Peter 1:3–8).

Call to Action

1. What are your primary values when looking for a local church?
2. How are you experiencing authentic, reciprocal relationships in your local church while supporting the vision of your local church?
3. Are you a member or a regular attendee? Why?
4. Would you say your commitment to your local church is more significant than your commitment to your job? What about your hobbies?
5. From your pastor's perspective, why is it essential for you to commit to the local church?

Are You Committed?

14

The Church Won't Help

I have a question about church discipline or how you handle a lack of church discipline or involvement from the church when trying to help someone. Though I don't have a current situation, it appears that church assistance should involve counsel, instruction, and, in some cases, the church's discipline to restore a brother or sister to Christ. What if this is not happening? Is there still a way to help those in need? How do you engage the church's help when the church isn't interested in following God's instruction? What if the person you are caring for knows the church isn't helping and loses heart for the church or disengages from the church?

—Supporting Member

A People Problem

First, I would reframe the discussion from a church problem to a people problem. Relabeling the questions makes it more personal and less abstract. To frame the discussion as a church issue can be vague enough to squirm away from personal responsibility, or unwisely condemn all churches when we know there are more good ones than bad ones. Of course, when you frame the discussion as a people problem, the first person you want to address is yourself.

Sometimes, we talk about the church like it is out there somewhere, as though we are not part of the problem we are discussing. What you do not want to do is to begin talking about them, those, and they as though we are not part of the problem. Personal ownership is where we want to evoke Matthew 7:3-5 into our frame of reference, so we do not self-righteously position ourselves above the problem while looking down on some vague entity, as though it's all about them.

Church Discipline?

The second thing to do is bring a more effective biblical contour to the words church discipline. This label was added to the Christian vocabulary by non-inspired people to highlight the church's responsibility toward those in need of corrective care. While I agree with the concept of discipline, I sometimes cringe at the process. Discipline—in the sense that some individuals use this word—is needed, but the goal of church discipline is always restoration. Therefore, a better term is church restoration or church discipline and restoration. Matthew 18:15-17 and Galatians 6:1-2 aim at the heart of this concept. The Matthew text tells you what to do—confront, and the Galatians text shows you how to do it—in a spirit of gentleness, hoping to restore an erring or hurting brother or sister.

The Galatian's text brings a spirit of governance to the directive in Matthew. Too often, people hang out in Matthew while ignoring the wisdom of Galatians. Christian discipleship without tears of compassion is neither Christian nor discipleship. You want your brothers and sisters to love you enough to bring corrective care, but you want them to do this in a spirit of gentleness.

The word restore in Galatians 6:1 is mending in Mark 1:19 and created in Hebrews 11:3. Church discipline will straighten you out, but church restoration will put you back together again. You want both of these things from your friends. All corrective care must be restorative in nature and goal.

The Church Won't

The church should be a significant player in sanctifying the body of Christ. Outside of personal responsibility and an individual's family, the church is the most considerable context the New Testament gives us to change, grow, and mature in Christ. Many of the New Testament letters were for local churches; they were written to assemblies or groups of people rather than to individuals. Paul, the chief writer of the New Testament, had a high view of the local church. He wrote to local communities with the expectation of the communities participating in the mutual sanctification of the individuals who made up each local assembly. Reciprocal soul care is assumed and expected. When it is not happening, what you have is an anomaly. It is a malignant body that cannot take care of itself. An inability to do soul care well drives at the heart of the question: what do you do when a local assembly has become malignant and is unwilling or unable to heal itself by taking care of its parts—its individual members? Is there a way to help these members?

Yes, there is. Most definitely. This problem is, in part, why our ministry exists. I am a para-church organization designed to come alongside—para—the church while not seeking to replace the church. Though you do not have to become a para-church organization like ours, you can still choose to equip the body of Christ as the Lord brings hurting people across your path. You can do one-to-one discipleship with any individual regardless of the inefficiency and ineffectiveness of a local church. The church should not control, hinder, or stop you from doing soul care. However, there is a downside: the more soul care you do, the more you will see the enormity of the problem, and the more you might complain. Helping others has several unintended consequences that can cause adverse outcomes:

- The more you do, the more you will care.
- The more you do, the more you will see.
- The more you do, the more frustrated you may become.
- The more you do, the more you will be tempted to force change on others and in your church.

I appeal not to perceive your growing awareness of church inefficiency as a negative but as a mercy from the Lord. He is allowing you to come in contact with more hurting people and permitting you to care enough about them to try to figure out how you can position yourself to where you can be most active in your local body.

What Do We Do

As you become more engaged with your church, you will want to motivate the church to become more intentional in its care of souls. This initiative has many more layers, and you must tread carefully. Thus, your starting point in this discussion must be the sovereignty of God. The Lord God Almighty is not sweating about this problem, even though it is real. No one can thwart His plans. He is in complete control of this issue in your church, and nothing will prevail against His plans for you and the rest of His body.

He is calm, cool, and collected (whatever that means), and you should be, too. If you are fretting, grumbling, or unwisely and uncharitably weighing in on this local church problem, you have jumped out on the wrong foot. You must bring your thoughts (and your feet) back under the care of our Sovereign Lord. God is in control. You must think about this problem from a position of faith in God, not fear of the perceived issues or ineffectiveness of a local church. God is at work, though He usually moves slower than you prefer.

The second thing to think about is not whether the local church will change but whether you will change. Are you doing all you can to make the church a better hospital for the wounded? Nobody has a right to complain about the church if they are not modeling what they want it to become. You have to decide what you want the church to become. If you do this, list what you want your church to become. After you make your list, please step back and look at it. Are you doing the things on the list? That is where you should begin. When I thought about this list, seven things popped into my mind. I want the church to be:

- A place where I can openly share my sins. Am I openly sharing my sins?
- A place that will not judge me. Do I uncharitably judge others?
- A place where I can come just as I am. Do I come just as I am, or am I pretentious?
- A place where I can take off my mask. Do I engage my church unmasked?
- A place where I can discuss my problems. Do I lead others by sharing my problems first?
- A place where the hurting receives care. Am I actively caring for the hurting?
- A place where small friend groups are like triage units. Am I laying myself bare in a small group of friends?

I only listed a few things necessary for authentic soul care to occur rather than listing everything I think a church should be doing to become a discipleship community.

Though this is not an exhaustive list, you get the idea. If you are not willing to be the things you want the church to become, you change first.

Love Thy Body

You hear people repeatedly say that there is no perfect church. You nod in the affirmative. Then you are disappointed by someone in the church. You are offended, or maybe the situation is direr: someone sins against you in the worst way imaginable. One of the most significant errors a person could make when sinned against is to disengage from the local church. Perhaps you should leave a specific local church, but you should not leave all local churches. You should find, join, and engage a local church. When hurt, permanent disengagement reflects more poorly on the person who rejects God's local church than on the local church.

I am not surprised when I hear about a local church doing bad things because local churches comprise evil people. While I do not condone bad people practices, and my heart breaks for the name of Christ and the souls left in the shambles of a poor church people experience, it is biblically illogical for a person to withdraw from the local church altogether. I do not think I need to make an argument for this because of the high view God places on the local church in the New Testament. The logic is akin to never revisiting a hospital because you had a bad experience in a hospital.

My desire is not to be callous or unsympathetic. I do believe I understand the problems, especially since my ministry is—more or less—a satellite station set up on the periphery of local church-ness to help hurting people. I engage many Christians who have wandered from, are in between, or are disenchanted with their local churches. Still, I am not leaving the local church because they do not do things well or according to my expectations or maybe even the way the Bible says they should. The local church is a God-ordained context for His children to do life together, and it will be that way until Jesus returns.

Find Two or Three

Some will argue, and it is a good argument, that I live in the southern part of the United States, where there is a church building on every street corner. We are probably more "church-i-fied" than any place outside Rome or Jerusalem. There are other regions in our world where finding solid believers is few and far between. A lack of local churches is a problem but not a show-stopper. A local church is not a white-frame building with a steeple on top of it. A local church is a body of believers.

You do not need a building to make a church. What you need are two or three believers. If that is all you have, that is where you should begin. But the main thing is you must guard your heart regarding your attitude and words when thinking about your local church. God's plan is working. It may not work according to how you want it to work, but He is writing the script, and you must make yourself comfortable with His story.

Call to Action

1. Is your church a discipleship community? If not, why not, and what is your plan to assist to make it better?
2. Are you a disciple-making individual? If not, why not?
3. Do you complain about your local church? If so, what is your plan to stop grumbling?
4. Are you guilty of some of the things that are in your complaints?
5. How must you change to make your church a better discipleship community? Will you begin by talking to one of your leaders?

15

How Do You Leave?

Sometimes, you can't stay at your local church. It's sad, but it happens all the time. You have to leave; when it happens, it's one of the more gut-wrenching seasons in any God-loving Christian's life. You love the Lord and His people, but for biblical and conscious reasons, and after gaining advice from helpful friends, the only option on the table is to find another local church. The good news is that there is a way to leave your church well. And there is a way to leave poorly.

Leaving Well

> I have been growing discontent with my church. I don't know how much of it is the church and how much of it is me. At this point, I'm not sure if I can resolve anything by communicating my concerns with the leadership. I am not one to church-hop. I have been in this church for nearly a decade, so I don't consider a change of churches lightly. At the same time, my area is not a Christian mecca, and I don't know if there is even a better option. Would it be wrong to start visiting other churches once a month or so to get a sense of other options while not severing

> my current connection? I have young children, and if I did seek out a different fellowship, I would want to make a transition as easy for them as possible.
> —Supporting Member

The question is, "How do you leave your church?" Well. That's it. You leave well. There is no other biblical alternative for leaving a local church but to leave the right way. Leaving well means you must be right with God. You must be right with others, as much as it depends upon you to work things out biblically (Romans 12:18). The counter to leaving well is to leave when your heart is not right with God or others. Those are not options. You do everything within your ability to leave on good terms. Leaving on good terms with every individual may be impossible in every situation, but you can be right with the Lord regardless of what others do, or how they respond. God should control your attitude and actions, not other people. He frees and empowers you to be right with Him while releasing you from harboring sin toward others.

Your attitude is the main thing to consider when thinking about leaving a local church. A proper attitude is how to end any relationship, whether with another person, your vocation, or your church. Having an ongoing sinful attitude toward other individuals or institutions is never right. If you leave on bad terms, ask the Lord to work in your heart so you can do as much as depends on you to make things right. I realize there are times when people leave on bad terms. It can work out this way when emotions are high, offenses happen, and uncharitable things are said. The good news is when things spin into an unresolvable disagreement, it does not have to stay that way.

> And Jesus said, "Father, forgive them, for they know not what they do."
> (Luke 23:34)

Minimally, you can change. An attitude of forgiveness is the power of the gospel that works in all God's children. The gospel has reconciling power. At some point, people should be able to work through sinful attitudes toward each other. The main point is that you can do right regardless of whether others follow your lead and pursue Christian charity and reconciliation.

Guard Thy Heart

Leaving well is imperative, and I want to drive this further home. Leaving a church is a big deal. No Christian should take this lightly. The Christian's life has three big spheres—family, work, and church. When you shake up any of these spheres, it's a serious matter, making it a challenge to be objective about what is happening to you. You love God's family, especially the family that makes up your local church. You commit to your church and have expectations of your local church. Sometimes, these expectations are unmet, and a person begins to think about leaving. When that happens, nobody is objective.

Still, you can leave with hurt and anger or go with grace. If you're in a situation where someone has offended you, the temptation will be to leave with the wrong attitude. Maybe you can't avoid leaving, but it would be wrong for you not to seek to gauge your heart. The biggest thing you'll struggle with regarding a sin issue will be self-righteousness, which is a greater than, better than attitude toward the church. Self-righteousness is looking down on others. In this case, it is looking down on your church—possibly the leaders or someone who has disappointed you within the congregation. A lofty position is a dangerous place to perch your heart.

> *Those who are well have no need of a physician, but those who are sick. I have not come to call the*

> righteous but sinners to repentance.
> (Luke 5:31–32)

There is no grace for the self-righteous person because Christ did not come to them. He came for the unrighteous, the needy, the hurting, and those who realize they are not better than anyone else. These humble servants want His mercy and grace. Apart from the grace of God, you are not better than any other person in the world. On your best day, you are equal to the human family. Without God imposing His grace into your life, you stand on level ground with the rest of us dirty, rotten sinners (1 Timothy 1:15). An angry, cocky, condescending, "I'm right, and you're wrong" attitude is not how any person should leave a church. Thus, the first place to begin is your heart.

> Search me, O God, and know my heart! Try me and know my thoughts! And see if there be any grievous way in me, and lead me in the way everlasting!
> (Psalm 139:23–24)

A Pastor's Perspective

When I pastored, there were times when a person or couple came to me and said, "We're leaving the church." They left. They did not leave with malice, as far as I know. They just left. My goal was never to keep a person in a place they did not want to be. It was never about our church being the only church. It was never about building a local kingdom or thinking, "We are the people." But I was a pastor. I cared for people, and while I never wanted to control people, I desired to serve them. It was always awkward for me when they would come to me and state their intentions but not ask for advice from me or anyone else.

Good shepherds shepherd, but when a person has decided to pack his bags, and the moving truck is at his door, there is nothing for me to say but, "May the Lord bless you and thanks for letting me know." It's not like I wanted to talk them out of leaving. I wanted to serve the exiting couple, but I also wanted to learn more about why they wanted to leave. In nearly every case, there was something for me to learn about myself and our church. Their departure was not only an opportunity to come alongside them, but they could come alongside us. I was not under the illusion we had the perfect church, and if a person was at the point of leaving, there was always something I could learn.

People leave churches because they like something better somewhere else. It would be arrogant of me to downplay their reasons for leaving while not humbly self-assessing how we could be a better church. This idea is another aspect of Matthew 7:3–5 — the log in my eye and a speck in yours. In this case, I applied it to our church. Rather than being critical about why they left, I judged the log in our eye by asking hard questions about our church—including the leadership. Perhaps they left for inadequate reasons. Those reasons did not hinder me from self-reflection on how to do church more effectively. Suppose your situation is not where you are comfortable sharing all your reasons for leaving or receiving counsel from your leaders. In that case, I recommend you receive guidance from other competent sources.

Don't Gossip

However, I do appeal to you if at all possible, to talk to your leaders about your intentions. If a person is thinking about leaving because the church has not met their expectations, others are probably thinking similarly. Your departure may be an opportunity to motivate the church to make some changes. Whatever you do, please don't gossip. Don't tell others about your disappointment unless the church is preaching heresy or there is abuse, or other comparable patterns, in the church.

If the church is a biblical church and the leadership humbly leads, they are doing some things right. They may not be doing it the way you want, but the gospel is going forth, and you can rejoice (Philippians 1:18). Other people do like your church, and the church is ministering to them. It's always like this. It works for some people, and it doesn't work for others. It would not serve other people to hear the downside of the church. Keep the circle tight regarding your critical opinion of your church—if it's a good church. There can be weak Christians in your congregation. There may also be those who are checking out the church. You don't want to cast unnecessary doubt in their minds. Again, we're not talking about heresy or sin being in play.

Gossip unnecessarily divides people, and if it's possible to keep division from happening in the body of Christ, do your part to keep it out of the church. When folks ask about your actions, let them know the Lord may lead you to another place. Keep it simple. You're not obliged to tell everyone more than that. If your peripheral friends press you, tell them what you love about your church, but remind them how the Lord is doing another kind of work in your heart.

Your Children

If you have children and they are young, they will hardly remember your church relocation. Children are resilient and have a great capacity to overcome challenges. But I would not recommend taking too long to make the decision. Your children need structure. If home, work, and church are the big three spheres for adults, then home, the church, and school are also the big three spheres for children. You could disrupt two out of their three primary contexts if you move. The potential for temporary upheaval does not mean you shouldn't move, but it does say that you don't want to drag things out for them.

They need security as much as anything right now, and a good church can partly provide this for them. Sit them down and talk to them about your plans—as much as is appropriate for their ages—if you visit other churches. You can remind them that the Lord is working in your hearts and that this is an excellent time to see what God is doing in other churches. Let them know you're not making a decision right now but only looking around perchance the Lord has something else for you all.

Reaffirm your love and protective care for them. Get their opinions, though staying or leaving should not be determined by their views. They are too young and will not be able to think about all the layers involved in this kind of decision, but you can allow them to be part of the family team by talking with them and removing as much mystery as possible. Insecurity—fear—will tempt your children. They need security and protection. Change can create instability. Stay close to them. Communicate with them. Reassure them about God's sovereign care.

Perfect Church

You know there is no perfect church. No clear-thinking Christian is under this illusion. Your next church will be a disappointment to some degree. Sin, sanctification, people, and a local church are four things that we cannot make right on this side of heaven. It's the sin piece that disrupts the entire fig cart. Make sure if you leave, your reason for leaving is biblical and a matter of conscience. As you visit other churches, scrutinize how they think about the gospel and their theology. These two things are the most essential pieces to any sound church.

Don't make this move about the children. Sometimes, parents can over-worry regarding their children and not trust the Lord to care for them. I was not in a church until I was 25 years old. Before coming to Christ, I was a hardcore pagan. I made it to Jesus via the jail. If your children make it to heaven, it will be because of the grace of God, not because of a perfect church. I know you know this. I'm only stating the obvious. The best gift you can give them is your prayers, followed by an unrelenting trust in God.

Think and pray robustly about this decision. If there is no heresy or sin in your local church, you may be in the best place you could be now. If your heart is free, live in God's freedom and make your decisions in God's freedom. It's not wrong to shop around. It's not wrong to leave a church. It may not be wrong to stay.

Call to Action

1. Do you like your church? Why or why not?
2. Do you want to leave over doctrine, sin, or preferences?
3. In what specific ways do you differ from your church leadership, and can you stay at your church, though you disagree?
4. In what ways have you contributed to the problems in your church?
5. In what ways have you contributed to making your church a more effective sanctification center?

16

Does He Groan?

What does your pastor think about when he thinks about you? Does that question sound strange to you? Perhaps you belong to a larger church where your pastor does not know you. Okay. But there is a leader at your church who does know you. What does that person think about when he thinks about you? My question is similar to what goes through your mind when you think about a special person in your life, perhaps a child. What I want to know is whether you are a joy to your pastor, a great, soul-searching query.

Think of Me

> Obey your leaders and submit to them, for they are keeping watch over your souls, as those who will have to give an account. Let them do this with joy and not with groaning, for that would be of no advantage to you.
>
> (Hebrews 13:17)

Perhaps you belong to a church but have not committed to that church. If that is the case, I appeal to you to make plans for a more substantial commitment to that local body so that your pastor can provide the people and contexts you need to receive care. I realize some folks will make an argument about the lack of New Testament emphasis on church membership. I understand and do not necessarily disagree with the perspective. But think about this for a minute.

Regardless of your perspective on church membership, does the person who exercises spiritual authority over you at your local church groan or expresses joy when he thinks about you? The writer of Hebrews tells Christians to let their pastors care for them with pleasure, not groaning. Unfortunately, in our modern buffet-style mentality, many Christians do not have a healthy, vibrant, and committed tethering to their local churches. Local church commitment for some folks works as efficiently as friending and unfriending on Facebook.

I commonly counsel people with low views and small commitments to their local churches. This kind of low view of the church invites sin into their lives because they miss out on a church's body-to-body ministries. It's not unusual to find a connection between low church commitment and personal or familial dysfunction. Paul wrote most of his letters to local churches. His appeals for sanctification were not primarily to individuals but to local churches. You can draw an accurate assumption from Paul's writings that Christians belonged and were committed to a local church. That is not true for some people nowadays.

Three Church Goers

THE UNDER-COMMITTED: If you attend a local church but your commitment is not active in that local church, I appeal to you to determine if your current church is for you. It might not be. But if it is the right church for you, please commit fully if you have not. One of the ways you can do this is by allowing them to care for you with joy, optimism, and gratitude. When I pastored, I found it especially difficult when someone came to our church but would not commit to it. It's like going into marriage with one foot out the door.

LOCAL CHURCH

Minor to no commitment to a local church is akin to a man who cuts his leg from his body while assuming it will survive. Or perhaps it's analogous to a divorced dad trying to parent his children every other weekend. Even if he wanted to parent his kids well, he would still be a part-time dad. These illustrations are self-sabotaging and abnormalities, but some Christians do not see anything wrong with spiritual disconnectedness from their local church.

THE COMMITTED: If you have a high view of the local church, evidenced by your consistent commitment to it, do you let your pastor care for you with joy? How do you know if he is full of joy or full of groaning when he thinks about you? How about if you ask your spiritual authority how he thinks about you? This kind of feedback gives you an excellent opportunity to serve your pastor, draw closer to each other, and cooperate together in impacting the rest of the body. Imagine if your child came to you and asked similar questions. Imagine if your child desired to bring joy to your life. "Hey Dad, do you parent me with joy?" Wouldn't that be awesome? Your pastor would feel identical if you sought to step up to that personal responsibility by asking these questions. The local church is like a "spiritual hospital." It is the God-ordained context where God's people can find spiritual help in their time of need. However, the local church is the sum of its parts, and if there are "parts" who don't commit to the local church, those "parts" will weaken the entire body.

THE FREE RADICALS: Free radicals are molecules that cause aging, tissue damage, and possibly diseases. These molecules are unstable. They look to connect with other molecules so that they can collectively destroy the vigor of the body—a detrimental process. Don't be a free radical. The uncommitted church attendee appears to be part of the local body but is not. Make your local church healthy by fully committing to it. If you need to reconsider your church because you're not sure it's the right fit, please type the word church in our search feature at LifeOverCoffee.com. We have scores of articles on the local church, including what to look for, how to leave, spiritual abuse, and so much more. Finding the right church is not a simple process, but it's worth the effort, and if you find it, jump in with both feet. The local church is the dearest place on earth besides our homes.

Call to Action

1. How would you rate your commitment to the local church? Why did you answer that way?
2. Will you pray over Hebrews 13:17, asking the Spirit to provide insight about you and your local church? What do you sense the Spirit is saying to you?
3. Will you share the ideas of this chapter and your "prayer thoughts" with your pastor or nearest spiritual mentor?
4. Will you ask that person what they think about when they think of you?
5. Specifically, ask them if you are a joy to care for and lead.

About the Author

Rick Thomas launched the Life Over Coffee global training network in 2008 to bring hope and help for you and others by creating resources that spark conversations for transformation. His primary responsibilities are resource creation and leadership development, which he does through speaking, writing, podcasting, and educating. In 1990 he earned a BA in Theology and, in 1991, a BS in Education. In 1993, he received his ordination into Christian ministry, and in 2000, he graduated with an MA in Counseling from The Master's University. In 2006, he was recognized as a Fellow of the Association of Certified Biblical Counselors (ACBC).

Other Books Available from Life Over Coffee

Boasting in Weakness
Centering Your Marriage on Christ
Communication
Complete Marriage
Don't Apologize
Exchange the Truth for a Lie
Help My Marriage Has Grown Cold
Identity Crisis
Local Church
Loving Me
Mad
Marriage Devotion We Are One
Politics and Culture
Parenting Devotion from Zero to Adulthood
Sex, Temptation, and Modesty
Storm Hurler
The Cyber Effect
The Talk
Wives Leading
You Decide

www.ingramcontent.com/pod-product-compliance
Lightning Source LLC
Chambersburg PA
CBHW052145070526
44585CB00017B/1978